Explore and Learn

volume 1

EARTH AND SPACE

land · oceans · earthquakes
volcanoes · mountains · water
weather · Earth · Sun · Moon
planets and stars · space travel

volume 2

SCIENCE AND TECHNOLOGY

materials · solids · gases · air · water
energy · magnetism · light and dark
communication · machines
buildings · the future

volume ►3◄

THE NATURAL WORLD

**seasons · plants · trees ·
fruits fungi · animals · insects
amphibians · reptiles · habitats
conservation**

volume 4

PEOPLE IN PLACE AND TIME

history · the world today · living
in different places · work · religion
movies, television and theater
sports · art · music

volume 5

ME AND MY BODY

people · families · the body · skeleton
muscles · blood · digestion · nerves
memories · sleeping · babies
growing old

volume 6

ATLAS OF THE WORLD

maps · climate · continents · homes in
different parts of the world · customs
language · food · flags · festivals
nationalities

ISBN 978-0-87197-482-2

M i l e s
K e L L y

SW
SOUTHWESTERN
advantage.

Produced by Miles Kelly Publishing Ltd
Harding's Barn, Bardfield End Green, Thaxted, Essex, CM6 3PX, UK

Printed by RR Donnelley, Shenzhen, Guangdong, China

Project Manager: Anne Marshall
Senior Editors: Belinda Gallagher, Lisa Regan
Assistant Editor: Helen Parker
Copy Editor: Jane Walker
Proofreader: Lyn Bresler
Indexer: Jane Parker
Senior Designer: Jo Cowan
Volume Designer: Sally Lace
Designer: Cathy May
Artwork Commissioning: Lynne French, Susanne Grant, Natasha Smith
Artwork Referencing: Lesley Cartlidge, Liberty Mella
Picture Research: Janice Bracken, Kate Miles
Production Controller: Rachel Jones
Art Director: Clare Sleven
Publishing Director: Jim Miles
Assets: Cathy Miles

Chief Executive Officer: Henry Bedford
President: Dan Moore
Curriculum Director: Janet D. Sweet
Art Director: Travis Rader
Production Manager: Powell Ropp

Color reproduction: DPI Colour, Saffron Walden, Essex

Specialist Consultants: Dr Belinda Ashon, Clive Carpenter, Janet Dyson MEd (education consultant), Tim Furniss (spaceflight journalist and author), Elysa Jacobs, Keith Lye BA, FRGS (geographical author and consultant), Steve Parker BSc (Scientific Fellow of the Zoological Society of London), Peter Riley BSc, Cbiol, MIBiol, PGCE (science writer and consultant), Sue Robson MA, PGCE (Senior Lecturer in education), Carol Watson (children's author)
Authors: Sally Hewitt, Steve Parker BSc (Scientific Fellow of the Zoological Society of London), Peter Riley BSc, Cbiol, MIBiol, PGCE, Philip Steele BA, Jane Walker BA
Stories: Karen Dolby BA
Projects: Vivienne Bolton
Project Photography: Alan Roberts

The publishers would also like to thank: Michelle Greenbank, Phil Kay, Cindy Leaney, Stoke College (Suffolk, UK), Fiona Greenland

volume 3
Explore and Learn
The Natural World

SOUTHWESTERN
advantage

Contents

All about your book   6

What is the natural world?   8

How seasons change   10

What is a plant?   12

Looking for simple plants   14

What is a flowering plant?   16

Why are shoots important?   18

Woody plants   20

Tree life   22

How plants live   24

Why do we grow plants?   26

Making seeds   28

What is a fruit?   30

Unusual plants   32

What is a fungus?   34

Who eats plants?   36

Animal life   38

Animals with skeletons   40

What is an insect?   42

Insect life   44

Soft, slimy animals   46

Eight-legged animals   48

Underwater animals 50

What is an amphibian? 54

What is a reptile? 56

Animals with feathers 58

Beaks and claws 60

What is a mammal? 62

Unusual mammals 64

In the ocean 66

On the seashore 68

In a river 70

Pond life 72

Living on grass 74

In the woods 76

Life in a rain forest 78

Rain forest birds 80

In the mountains 82

In the desert 84

Do animals live on ice? 86

Why do we need wildlife parks? 88

Can you remember? 90

Index 92

All about your book

Explore and Learn **will take you on a journey of discovery.**
Its six volumes will lead you through the world of plants and animals, into science and technology, explaining how things work and why. It will tell you about the world you live in and the universe beyond Earth. It will also help you discover new and wonderful things about yourself and the people around you.

Thumb index This is a guide to what each page contains. If you turn the pages quickly you will easily be able to find the subjects you are interested in.

Volume button This tells you which volume you are looking at. Here is the Earth and Space button that explores our world.

exploring
Think, find, research, act out—these boxes help you to discover more about what you have read on a page. See if your family and friends can help you with some of these activities and ideas.

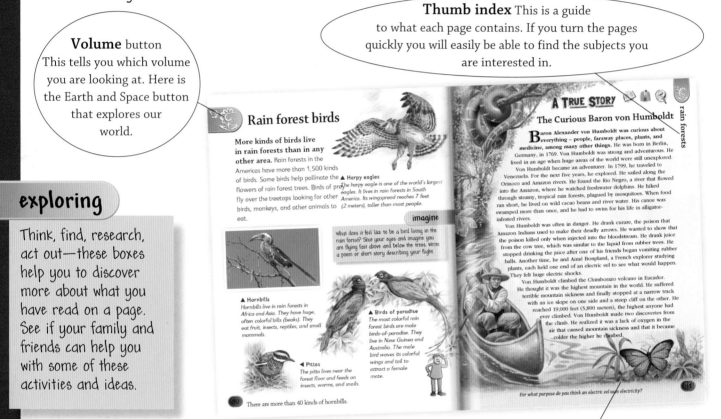

Rain forest birds

More kinds of birds live in rain forests than in any other area. Rain forests in the Americas have more than 1,500 kinds of birds. Some birds help pollinate the flowers of rain forest trees. Birds of prey fly over the treetops looking for other birds, monkeys, and other animals to eat.

▲ **Harpy eagles**
The harpy eagle is one of the world's largest eagles. It lives in rain forests in South America. Its wingspread reaches 7 feet (2 meters), taller than most people.

imagine
What does it feel like to be a bird living in the rain forest? Shut your eyes and imagine you are flying fast above and below the trees. Write a poem or short story describing your flight.

▲ **Hornbills**
Hornbills live in rain forests in Africa and Asia. They have huge, often colorful bills (beaks). They eat fruit, insects, reptiles, and small mammals.

◄ **Pittas**
The pitta lives near the forest floor and feeds on insects, worms, and snails.

▲ **Birds of paradise**
The most colorful rain forest birds are male birds-of-paradise. They live in New Guinea and Australia. The male bird waves its colorful wings and tail to attract a female mate.

There are more than 40 kinds of hornbills.

A TRUE STORY
The Curious Baron von Humboldt

Baron Alexander von Humboldt was curious about everything – people, faraway places, plants, and medicine, among many other things. He was born in Berlin, Germany, in 1769. Von Humboldt was strong and adventurous. He lived in an age when huge areas of the world were still unexplored.
Von Humboldt became an adventurer. In 1799, he traveled to Venezuela. For the next five years, he explored. He sailed along the Orinoco and Amazon rivers. He found the Rio Negro, a river that flowed into the Amazon, where he watched freshwater dolphins. He hiked through steamy, tropical rain forests, plagued by mosquitoes. When food ran short, he lived on wild cacao beans and river water. His canoe was swamped more than once, and he had to swim for his life in alligator-infested rivers.
Von Humboldt was often in danger. He drank curare, the poison that Amazon Indians used to make their deadly arrows. He wanted to show that the poison killed only when injected into the bloodstream. He drank juice from the cow tree, which was similar to the liquid from rubber trees. He stopped drinking the juice after one of his friends began vomiting rubber balls. Another time, he and Aimé Bonpland, a French explorer studying plants, each held one end of an electric eel to see what would happen. They felt huge electric shocks.
Von Humboldt climbed the Chimborazo volcano in Ecuador. He thought it was the highest mountain in the world. He suffered terrible mountain sickness and finally stopped at a narrow track with an ice slope on one side and a steep cliff on the other. He reached 19,000 feet (5,800 meters), the highest anyone had ever climbed. Von Humboldt made two discoveries from the climb. He realized it was a lack of oxygen in the air that caused mountain sickness and that it became colder the higher he climbed.

For what purpose do you think an electric eel uses electricity?

You might choose to read each book from beginning to end, or you might decide to look up things that interest you in the index that appears at the end of each book. All the different features have been created to help you learn, discover, and have fun finding out. You might just enjoy turning each page and looking at all the wonderful pictures showing life and the world around you.

Stories
You can find stories that come from different countries all over the world. Some are myths, others are fables, and some are taken from the Bible. How much can you remember? See if you can answer the questions that appear at the end of each story.

Fun facts Amazing, true facts that will surprise you and your friends.

Curriculum buttons

English   Math   Science   History   Geography   Art   Music   Design and technology   Information technology

Curriculum buttons These help you figure out which subjects are covered on each page. Do you like history? If so, you can turn the pages and read about history wherever you see the history button. Or maybe you like to draw. Watch for the art button or the design and technology button. Do you enjoy reading? Watch for the English button.

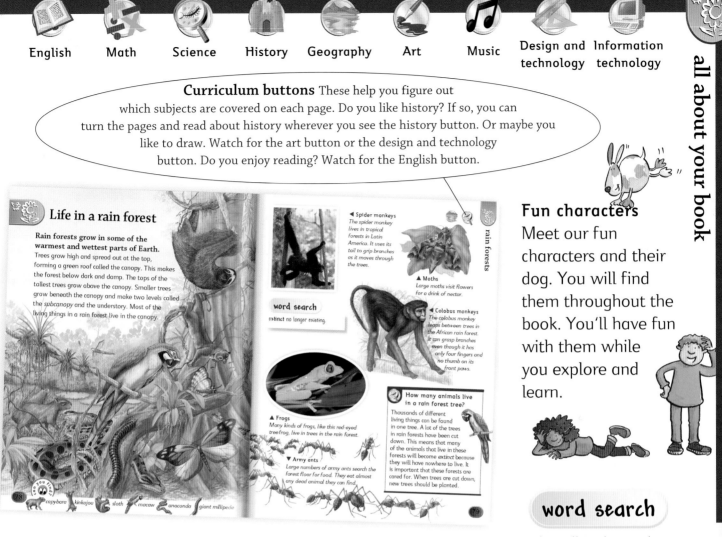

Life in a rain forest

Rain forests grow in some of the warmest and wettest parts of Earth. Trees grow high and spread out at the top, forming a green roof called the canopy. This makes the forest below dark and damp. The tops of the tallest trees grow above the canopy. Smaller trees grow beneath the canopy and make two levels called the *subcanopy* and the understory. Most of the living things in a rain forest live in the canopy.

word search
extinct no longer existing.

◄ **Spider monkeys**
The spider monkey lives in tropical forests in Latin America. It uses its tail to grip branches as it moves through the trees.

▲ **Moths**
Large moths visit flowers for a drink of nectar.

◄ **Colobus monkeys**
The colobus monkey leaps between trees in the African rain forest. It can grasp branches even though it has only four fingers and no thumb on its front paws.

rain forests

▲ **Frogs**
Many kinds of frogs, like this red-eyed treefrog, live in trees in the rain forest.

▼ **Army ants**
Large numbers of army ants search the forest floor for food. They eat almost any dead animal they can find.

How many animals live in a rain forest tree?
Thousands of different living things can be found in one tree. A lot of the trees in rain forests have been cut down. This means that many of the animals that live in these forests will become *extinct* because they will have nowhere to live. It is important that these forests are cared for. When trees are cut down, new trees should be planted.

78   capybara   kinkajou   sloth   macaw   anaconda   giant millipede   79

Fun characters

Meet our fun characters and their dog. You will find them throughout the book. You'll have fun with them while you explore and learn.

word search

This will explain and give the meaning of some new or difficult words that are used on a page. You can test yourself to see if you can spell the words and know what they mean. See if you can find where they appear on the page.

What is the answer?

Do you know? Read on and find out. These boxes will help you learn more about history, geography, science, and other subjects. A **curriculum button** appears at the top beside the question. This tells you what subject is covered. You can choose whatever boxes you are most interested in to read about.

Projects

You can draw, paint, and build all sorts of different things. You will find a list of everything you will need to make each project. Carefully follow the step-by-step instructions that tell you how to do each project. Ask an adult for help with some of the more difficult steps.

Wild woods

How many creatures can you spot? Cut out and paint your own owls, butterflies, and birds to live in your forest.

You will need
· cardboard box · pencil
· glue and brush · paints and paintbrush · tape
· 6 sheets of construction paper · scissors

❶ On each sheet of paper, draw trees, plants, and bushes. Paint these scenes and cut around them carefully. Glue on your animals and birds. Cut out one side of the box and a hole in the top.

❷ Using tape, attach the layers of paper inside the box, one in front of the other. Watch the light shine through the top of the box. How many of your animals can you see peering through the trees?

Find out more about forests and trees on pages 20, 21, 22, and 23.   77

Children should be assisted in using certain tools and undertaking particular tasks. Children should not be left unsupervised to carry out these projects.

What is the natural world?

The natural world is the world of living things and their natural surroundings. There are two main kinds of living things. They are plants and animals. You can find them in almost every place on Earth. Some living things are found on the floor of the deepest oceans. Others float or fly through the air above the clouds. In between the deep ocean and the sky is the land, with its forests, deserts, lakes, and rivers. All these places are part of the natural world.

▶ **In the ocean**
Billions of tiny plants and animals live in the water near the surface of the ocean. They drift in the ocean currents and are called plankton.

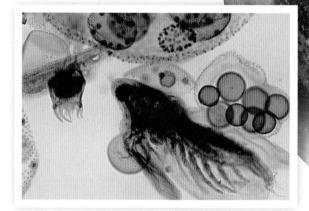

word search

currents movement of water in a river or in the ocean.
planet a huge, round object that moves around a star.

▶ **Deepest oceans**
Rattail fish live at the bottom of the deepest oceans. They feed on shrimps and worms that they find on the ocean floor.

▼ In the air

A spider makes a silk streamer. The wind blows and lifts the streamer and spider into the air. Some very small spiders are lifted into the clouds, then sink to the ground and spin a web.

Is there life in seas on other planets?

The planet Jupiter has more than 65 moons. One is called Europa. It is covered in ice. There may be a sea of water beneath Europa's ice. Such a sea could be home to different kinds of living things.

◄ The Earth

The only place that we know where plants and animals live.

▼ Life on land

These plants and animals live in Africa. It is the large piece of land you can see in the right of the picture of Earth.

count

How many animals and plants can you think of? Ask one of your friends to count up the names as you say them.

9

How seasons change

The weather is not the same every day of the year. In many places, there are four seasons each year. They are spring, summer, autumn, and winter. Each season has different weather. In summer it is hot, but in winter it is cold. The change in the weather is due to the way Earth moves around the sun. Many plants and animals can stay alive through all the seasons by changing how they live. Some animals change where they live, too.

▲ **Spring**
In spring, the weather gets warmer, plants make flowers, trees grow new leaves, and birds make nests and lay eggs.

When a part of Earth tilts toward the sun, it is summer there.

▲ **Summer**
In summer, many insects fly through the air or crawl on the ground looking for food. Many plants start to make fruits and seeds. Young animals such as rabbits and deer grow up quickly.

▼ Winter

Many animals hide from the cold and enter a sleeplike state in winter. Some frogs in Canada spend the winter frozen in ice.

▼ The seasons

Earth moves around the sun once every year. Earth is tilted as it moves. Both the movement and the tilt make the seasons.

▶ Autumn

In autumn, the weather gets cooler. Some trees lose their leaves. Insects die but leave eggs hidden safely for next year.

When the same part of Earth tilts away from the sun, it is winter there.

Scientists have found hundreds of thousands of kinds of plants.

What is a plant?

If you watch a plant, you may think it does not move, but you would be wrong. A plant moves very slowly as it grows. Its shoot grows up into the air, and its root grows down through the soil. Some plants keep growing most of their lives. Very old plants can be very large. Most plants can do something that animals cannot do. They can make their own food in the green parts of their bodies. In most plants, these parts are the leaves and stems. Some plants are tiny, and you need a special instrument called a microscope to see them. Other plants are many times taller than you.

▶ **The largest plants**
The tallest trees in the world are redwood trees that grow in North America. Their trunks can grow to about 12 feet (3.7 meters) thick and reach a height of 300 feet (90 meters) or more. Some redwoods can live longer than 2,000 years.

measure

Plant a small onion in a pot of compost. Water it when the top of the soil is dry. Each day, measure how much the shoot has grown.

◀ **Is it a plant?**
Algae *are simple organisms that live in water and moist soil. Some people think they are plants, but they are not. Like plants, algae can make their own food.*

◀ **Flowering plants**
Flowering plants make up the largest group of plants. The stem, leaves, and flowers all come from the shoot, which grows above the ground.

word search

algae simple plantlike organisms.
minerals materials found in the soil that help plants to grow and stay healthy.
shoot the young part of a plant that you can see growing above the ground.

leaf

shoot

seed

root

▶ **Roots for feeding**
Most plants have roots that grow through the soil and take in water and minerals.

▶ **Roots for strength**
The roots of this palm tree hold it firmly in the ground when a strong wind blows.

Looking for simple plants

Simple plants do not have flowers, but they may have roots, stems, and leaves. When a simple plant is fully grown, it makes tiny cases called *spores*. Inside each spore is a small piece of the plant. The spores leave the plant and drift through the air or water. When the spore reaches a suitable new place, it breaks open. The part of the plant inside the spore grows out and makes a new plant. Some mosses only grow as high as your little finger, but some ferns can grow taller than you.

▼ **Woodlands**
Many kinds of simple plants can be found growing in a woodland area. They like the damp, shady conditions under the tall trees. Many also grow around woodland pools.

▼ Ferns
The fern stem grows underground. It forms leaf-like parts above ground. These are called fronds. When the frond starts to grow from the stem, it uncurls and looks like a walking stick. Later, spores form in brown lumps on the underside of the frond.

◄ Horsetails
Horsetails make two kinds of stems. In early spring, they grow stems with a cone at the top. The cone makes spores that float away in the air. Later, horsetails grow leafy stems that look like they are covered with small, upside-down umbrellas.

▶ Liverworts
Some liverworts look like mosses (below). Others have a waxy green body that lies flat on the ground and is shaped like a tongue. Many liverworts may grow together.

When mosses and liverworts are ready to make spores, they grow stalks. The tip of each stalk swells and the spores form inside. The tip breaks open to let out the spores.

▲ Mosses
Mosses often form soft, thick mats on rocks, trees, and soil. Most mosses grow in moist, shady places. Mosses have short stems covered with tiny leaves. Threadlike parts hold the plants in place.

15

What is a flowering plant?

A flowering plant grows from a seed.
When the seed is warm and damp, it sprouts a root and then a shoot. The root and shoot are the two main parts of a flowering plant. The shoot grows into the stem, leaves, and flowers. There are more flowering plants than all other plants put together. You can identify each one by the shape and color of its flowers and leaves. The flower helps the plant to produce new plants by making pollen and seeds. Insects also help by carrying the pollen from flower to flower (see page 28).

▲ **Seedling**
A seed takes in water from damp ground and a tiny seedling grows out of it. As the seedling gets bigger, flowers develop on its stem.

bud

flower

word search

pollen a powder that plants need to make seeds.
seed contains the parts to grow a tiny flowering plant.
seedling the small young plant that grows out of a seed.

stem

leaf

root

16

▼ Many flowers

Some flowering plants have many flowers growing on one stem.

floret

▲ Flower head

This is a flower head. It is made up of many tiny flowers called florets.

▼ Inside a flower

This close-up picture shows the petals *and* stamens *of a flower. Hidden inside is the* ovary, *where seeds grow.*

Petals are brightly colored and have a scent that attracts insects to the flower.

Stamens have tips that produce pollen.

Why are shoots important?

The two main parts of the shoot are the leaves and the stem. The leaves make food by using sunlight. The stem acts as a support for the leaves by holding them up to the sun so it can shine on them. The food made in the leaves moves through narrow tubes in the stem. It goes to all parts of the plant, especially those that are growing. Growing parts are the tips of the shoot and root, new buds, and flowers.

▲ Weak stems
Ivy has a weak, flexible stem that needs support. It often climbs up tree trunks and walls. Some ivy creeps along the ground.

◀ Woody stems
Some stems are extremely strong and stiff because they are made of wood. A trunk is the main woody stem of a tree. This picture shows a tree in the rain forest.

◀ Spiny stems
Stems and leaves may have special parts to help plants stay alive. The stem of the gorse plant has sharp spines that prevent animals from eating it.

word search

rain forest a thick forest where there is a lot of rainfall.

whorl leaves growing in a ring around a stem.

▼ **Patterns of leaves on a stem**

Leaves grow on a stem in a pattern to help them catch the sunlight. They may grow in pairs **1**. *They may grow in a ring, called a whorl, around the stem* **2**. *Some leaves are arranged one after another along a stem* **3**.

1

examine

Look at the plants that grow in your home. Examine how the leaves are arranged on the stems of each one.

AN ABORIGINAL MYTH

Above the Oobi-Oobi Mountain

Long ago, the tribes of Australia fought a terrible battle. The flowers were so sad they turned brown and died. Blossoms fell from the trees. No new flowers grew, and people missed them. Finally, one man from each tribe was sent to the All-Seeing Spirit for help. They climbed up and up to the top of the high Oobi-Oobi Mountain. The Spirit saw the tired men and lifted them above the clouds, where flowers grew in all the colors of the rainbow.

"Pick as many as you can," said the Spirit. "Take them back to your tribes and tell them flowers will grow again as long as they live together peacefully."

What had the tribes done wrong? Who lifted the men above the clouds?

19

Woody plants

Trees provide us with one of the most useful materials to be found on Earth—wood. Tree trunks are covered in bark. Bark protects trees from being eaten by animals and from harsh weather conditions such as the cold of winter. Trees can be divided into two groups by the shape of their leaves and the way that they make seeds. Trees that have wide, flat leaves and make seeds in flowers are called broad-leaved trees. Trees that have long, narrow leaves and make seeds in cones are *conifers*.

▲ **Autumn leaves**
In autumn, leaves change color before they drop off trees and fall to the ground.

▼ **Leaflets**
Some leaves, like those of the ash tree, are so large that they are divided into leaflets.

▲ **Tree rings**
Many trees grow a new layer of wood each year. If you cut the tree down, these layers appear as rings in the trunk. The number of rings can tell you how old the tree is.

word search

evergreen a tree that always has leaves.
leaflets parts of a large leaf sharing the same stalk.

1 **2**

▲ Fir cones

Conifers have two kinds of cones. One kind makes seeds **1** *and the other kind makes pollen* **2**.

Do all trees grow the same wood?

Every type of tree grows a different kind of wood. Some trees grow strong wood and some grow light wood. These woods are used for different things. Pine wood grows fast and is quite strong. It is used to make furniture. Ash wood is stiff and light and is ideal for broom handles. Balsa wood is very light and is used to make model planes.

▼ Shrubs and bushes

These are shorter than trees. Their branches grow outward near the ground.

◄ Conifers

These trees lose some of their leaves all year round and grow new ones right away. They always have some leaves and so are called evergreen trees.

▲ Broad-leaved trees

Most broad-leaved trees lose their leaves in autumn or the dry season. They grow new ones the following spring or wet season.

The oldest living tree is a bristlecone pine in California. It is 4,600 years old.

Tree life

Trees are like tall apartment buildings and supermarkets for animal life. Insects burrow in the wood. Birds and mammals feed on a tree's fruits and make nests in its branches.

▲ **Life in a rain forest**
Plants, frogs, and snakes live among the branches of rain forest trees.

▼ **Life in a conifer**
Chipmunks and squirrels feed on the seeds in a conifer's cones. An owl may roost in the branches until dark.

▲ **Life in a broad-leaved tree**
Beetles live in the bark of a broad-leaved tree, and woodpeckers feed on them. Aphids feed on the leaves and are eaten by warblers. A crow may nest in the treetop.

look

Stand under a tree and look up at the leaves. Can you see insects on the leaves?

Owl collage

Look closely at this collage.

Can you see a wise old owl peering out through the leaves and flowers?

1 Gather some leaves and flowers and press them between the pages of a heavy book. Also dry some leaves loose. They will become all sorts of interesting shapes. Gather moss, feathers, and pieces of bark and twigs to frame your collage.

You will need

- construction paper · dried moss · feathers
- pressed leaves and flowers · felt marker
- pieces of bark and twigs · glue

2 Draw an owl on the construction paper, then spread glue over the picture.

3 Glue the flowers, leaves, moss, and feathers just on the owl. Arrange a border of leaves around the edge.

23

How plants live

Plants live in a very different way from animals. Most plants can make their own food from sunlight, air, and water in the soil. Plants begin making food in the morning when the sun rises and finish when the sun sets. They open tiny holes on the surface of their leaves and take in a gas called *carbon dioxide* from the air. They use this gas and water to make their food. Plants also make oxygen when they make food. They release the oxygen from their leaves into the air. Most living things need oxygen to stay alive.

▲ **Plants need water.**
Leaves have a coat of wax. Rainwater cannot get through it. The water must go into the soil and be sucked up into the plant by its roots.

▶ **Plants need light.**
Plants grow well around the mouth of the cave, but they do not grow inside it. There is not enough light in the cave for the plants to make food.

grow

Plant a seedling. Water it and put the pot near a window. See how the seedling grows toward the light.

word search

crop a large number of plants of one kind grown for human use.

fertilizer a rich mixture of minerals and other substances that helps plants to grow.

▲ **Plants make oxygen.**
When water plants make food, they give off bubbles containing oxygen.

▲ **Plants need minerals.**
When plants and animals die, their bodies rot and release natural substances called minerals *into the soil. The minerals enter living plants through their roots and help the plants grow. Farmers sometimes add extra minerals to their crops by putting fertilizer on the soil.*

Rainbow flowers

If you would like to create unusual colored flowers, try this experiment.

You will need

- white chrysanthemum or carnation · knife
- two colors of food coloring
- two clear glasses

Ask an adult to carefully split the flower stem using a knife. Partly fill each glass with water and a few drops of food coloring. Use a different color of food coloring in each glass. Place one half of the stem in each glass. After an hour, you will see the different colors creeping into the flower petals.

Why do we grow plants?

Almost all our food comes from plants.

Bread is made from wheat, and sugar comes from sugarcane or beets. Even milk comes from the grass that cows eat. The main reason we grow plants is to eat them and to feed other animals. But we also grow plants for their *fiber* and for decoration. Fibers are hairlike strands that can be made into clothing. Many people decorate their homes and yards with attractive plants.

▶ **Plants for eating**

Plants are grown in different countries all over the world. Have you eaten these tropical fruits and vegetables?

1 *avocado*
2 *papaya*
3 *guava*
4 *mango*
5 *pepper*
6 *sweet potato*
7 *yam*

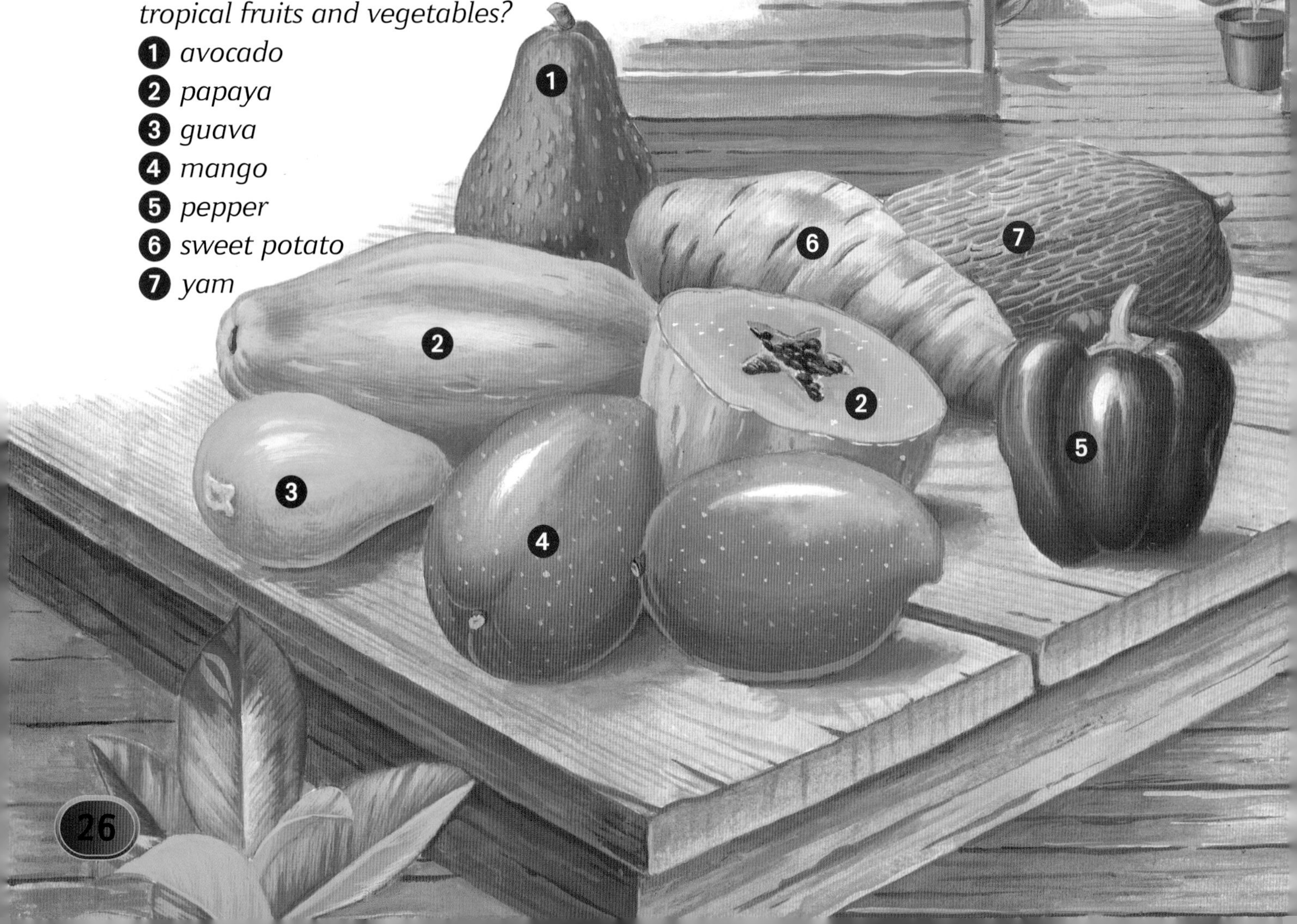

chilies

garlic

thyme

mint

cinnamon

coriander
seeds

▲ Plants for flavor

Some plants are grown to provide seasoning for food. Do you recognize any of these flavorful seasonings?

Do you eat these foods?

cabbage | green onions

peppers | carrots

tomatoes | potatoes

▶ Caring for plants

Houseplants need light, warmth, and water so that they stay healthy.

▼ Plants for decoration

There are many plants that people grow at home. They may be grown for the shape and color of their leaves or the brightness of their flowers.

look after

Read the care instructions for the plants in your home. Make a list of all the things that a plant needs to remain healthy. Try looking after the plants yourself.

Some people have cactus houseplants. They need watering less than other plants.

Making seeds

stamens

Flowers make a yellow dust called pollen so that they can produce seeds.
Many flowers also make a sweet juice called *nectar*. Insects land on flowers and feed off the nectar. They pick up pollen on their hairy bodies. The pollen sticks to an insect when it flies away. When the insect visits another flower, it may transfer pollen to a sticky part of that flower called the *stigma*. When pollen has been moved from one flower to another like this, *pollination* has happened. The second flower has been fertilized. Some flowers are pollinated by the wind.

▼ Wind pollination
Grasses and willows are pollinated by the wind. Their flowers are small and do not have petals. They are packed together in a group and the stamens stick out into the air.

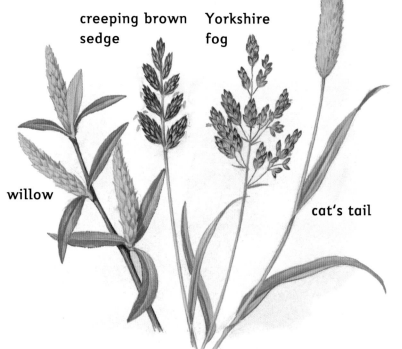

creeping brown sedge

Yorkshire fog

willow

cat's tail

▼ Insect pollination

A bee visits a flower for a drink of nectar and picks up pollen from the flower's stamens. The bee then travels to another flower to find more nectar. The pollen that it picked up in the first flower sticks to the second flower's stigma.

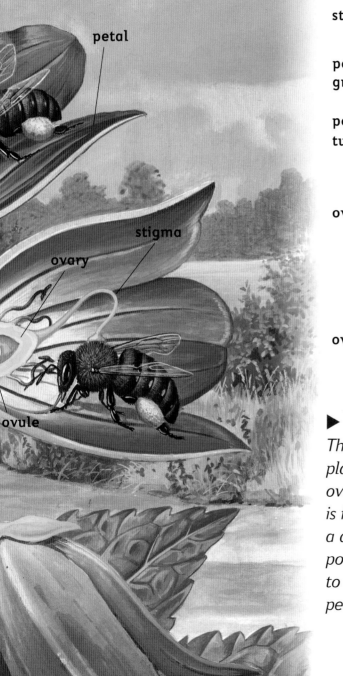

petal

stigma

ovary

ovule

word search

fertilization part of the process of making a seed to produce new plants.

nectar a juice made from sugar and water.

pollination the moving of pollen from one flower to another.

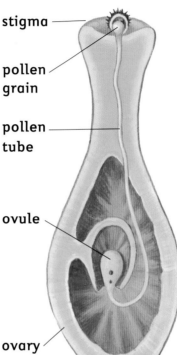

stigma

pollen grain

pollen tube

ovule

ovary

◄ The ovary

Under the stigma is the ovary. A pollen grain on the stigma grows a tube into the ovary. The tube grows to a part of the ovary called the ovule. When the tube reaches the ovule a substance in the pollen tube joins with a substance in the ovule. This is called fertilization.

▶ Pea seeds

The ovary of a pea plant has many ovules. Each one is fertilized by a different pollen grain to make a pea seed.

find

Look inside a pea pod and count the seeds. Can you find a little ovule that has not been fertilized?

The smallest flowering plant is a duckweed. Its flowers are as tiny as pinheads.

What is a fruit?

Plants do not grow flowers for us to enjoy their colors and scents. A plant grows flowers to make seeds, which grow into more plants. A fruit is the part of a plant containing seeds. The seeds must travel far enough from the plant so they have room to grow. The wind and animals help seeds travel by carrying away the fruits that contain them.

▲ Fruits with wings
The maple tree has a fruit with a wing. When the wind blows on the wing, it carries the fruit away from the tree to grow in a new place.

▼ Berries
Many fruits have juicy parts that animals eat. The animal eats the seeds inside the fruit. The hard seeds pass through its body unharmed.

◀ Fruits with parachutes
Dandelion fruits are shaped like parachutes. The wind blows them into the air. The fruits may travel long distances in the wind before they fall to the ground.

▲ Hooks
The burdock fruit grows hooks. These stick to animals' fur as they brush past. This fox is carrying burdock fruits away on its body.

gather

Find and gather some parachute fruits like the dandelion's. How far do they travel when you blow them? How high do they rise?

30

Tropical fruit bowl

What is your favorite fruit? Maybe it is pineapple or a peach. This delicious-looking fruit is not for eating, but it will look colorful on your table.

You will need

- newspaper • old bowl
- glue and brush • cooking oil
- different colored paints

1 Make rough fruit shapes from scrunched-up newspaper. Water down the glue and use it to stick five layers of newspaper over the shapes. Leave them in a warm, airy spot to dry.

2 Brush the outside of the bowl with the oil. Glue six layers of newspaper strips to the bowl to make a strong mold. Let this dry overnight.

3 Once the fruit shapes are dry, paint them in realistic colors.

4 Separate your dried newspaper mold from the old bowl. Decorate the mold in bright, tropical colors. When the paint is dry, put your fruit shapes in it.

Unusual plants

Some plants are killers! They catch insects for extra food. These plants grow in soil where they do not get enough minerals. They get the minerals they need by feeding on insects. Some flowering plants make their own food and also take some from other plants. A few plants steal all their food and hardly look like plants at all.

▲ Stealing food
The dodder does not have any leaves to make food. It lives by taking all it needs from the plants on which it grows. It only looks like a plant when it grows flowers.

◄ Drowned
The leaf of a pitcher plant grows into a long, hollow tube. The bottom of the tube fills with water. The leaf has a smell that attracts insects. They climb inside the leaf to look for nectar and fall into the water and drown. The plant feeds on their dead bodies.

32

—

▶ Stuck

The sundew has hairy leaves. Insects get caught in sticky drops on the tips of the hairs. The plant slowly feeds on the soft parts of the insects' bodies. The wind blows away such hard body parts as the legs and wings.

▼ Trapped

The leaves of the Venus's-flytrap are divided into two halves. When insects land on them, they snap together like a trap. Spines on the leaves' edges act like prison bars and prevent the insects from escaping.

▶ Mistletoe living on wood

Birds eat the mistletoe fruit, and the seeds stick to their beaks. When the birds sharpen their beaks by rubbing them on another tree, the seeds get stuck in the bark. When the seeds sprout, they grow leaves to make food. They also take food from inside the tree trunk.

Some large pitcher plants can trap and digest birds or lizards.

What is a fungus?

A fungus is not a plant or an animal.

It belongs to a group of living things called *fungi*. The body of a fungus is made of many threads, like those in cotton balls. The threads grow as they feed. Like simple plants, fungi make spores. When a spore breaks open, a fungus grows out of it and starts to feed on plants and animals. Most fungi feed on dead plants and animals, helping them to rot and form minerals in the soil. Some fungi feed on living plants and animals.

▶ **Toadstools**
As young toadstools sprout and begin to grow, the edges of their caps begin to separate from their stalks.

◀ **Tree fungus**
Some kinds of fungi grow inside tree stumps. They have threads that feed on the dead wood. When the threads have grown through the wood, they make toadstools on the outside of the stump.

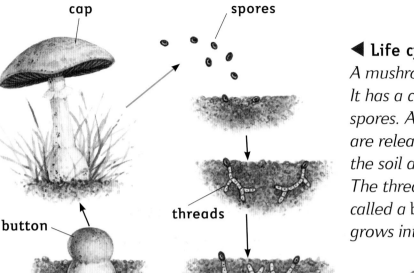

cap

spores

button

threads

◀ Life cycle of a fungus

A mushroom is a fungus. It has a cap that makes spores. After the spores are released, they land in the soil and grow threads. The threads make a lump called a button. *The button grows into a mushroom.*

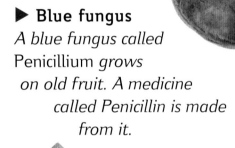

▶ Blue fungus

A blue fungus called Penicillium *grows on old fruit. A medicine called Penicillin is made from it.*

◀ Fungus on wheat

Fungi called rusts *grow on living plants and take food from their leaves. Rusts and other fungi called* mildews *are pests because they can ruin whole fields of crops.*

microscopic view

word search

microscopic so small that it can only be seen by using a special instrument called a microscope that makes things look bigger.

spore a tiny piece of fungus or simple plant with a hard coating around it.

Who eats plants?

You eat plants, and so do other animals. A plant may have animals nibbling at its roots, chewing on its leaves, and drinking the nectar from its flowers. Animals that feed chiefly on plants are called *herbivores*. They may be as small as a caterpillar or as large as an elephant. Some animals, such as bears and many monkeys, eat plants and other animals. They are called *omnivores*. Human beings belong to this group of feeders. Some animals prefer to feed on other animals instead of plants. They are called *carnivores*.

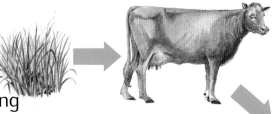

▲ Food production
You are part of many food chains. When you drink milk, you belong to a food chain.

▲ Elephants
Elephants pull down high branches with their trunks to reach the leaves.

▼ Short food chain
Animals can be linked together by the way they feed. The way they are linked together is called a food chain. *Herbivores such as mice feed on plants, and carnivores such as owls feed on mice.*

think

Can you think of some food chains in which you are a link? Start by thinking about the fruits and vegetables you eat.

word search

carnivore an animal that feeds mainly on animals.
herbivore an animal that feeds mainly on plants.
omnivore an animal that feeds on plants and animals.

▼ Lions
Lions are carnivores. They eat zebras and gnus (wildebeests) that feed on grass.

▼ Rabbits
Rabbits are herbivores. They snip off grass leaves with their front teeth.

AN AESOP FABLE

The Grasshopper and the Ants

It was the hottest of hot summers, and all day and every day the ants worked hard. They carried seeds and grain, nuts and fruit, down through tunnels in their anthill to fill their food store far below ground. Grasshopper lazed in the sun, playing his chirruping song. He was happy, without a care in the world.

Then summer turned to autumn and the wind began to blow. The sky clouded over. There was no warm sunshine. Grasshopper was cold and hungry. He remembered the busy ants and their stock of food.

Shivering, he knocked on the door of the anthill.

"Please, will you give me something to eat?" he asked.

"Why should we?" said the ants. "You spent the summer singing while we worked and made stores for the long winter months ahead."

What should Grasshopper do next year? Should the ants share their food?

Animal life

Most animals can move from place to place and take in food. Most plants cannot do these things. Scientists believe there are millions of different kinds of animals. The largest animal in the world is the blue whale, which can grow to 100 feet (30 meters) long. That's about as long as five elephants in a row! The smallest animals are so tiny that you need a microscope to see them. Animals can be divided into two main groups. These are *vertebrates,* which have backbones, and *invertebrates,* which do not.

jellyfish

ragworm   sea slug

▲ Soft bodies
Some invertebrates, like the common jellyfish, have soft bodies. They keep their shape because of the water inside and around them.

▼ The largest animal
The blue whale is a vertebrate living in the sea. It feeds mainly on small, shrimplike animals called krill. *The blue whale eats huge numbers of krill and may have 2 tons (1.8 metric tons) of krill in its stomach after a meal.*

word search

invertebrates animals without backbones.
vertebrates animals with backbones.

stag beetle

lobster

▲ **Hard bodies**
These invertebrates have hard bodies and legs with many joints. Stag beetles live on land. Lobsters live in the ocean.

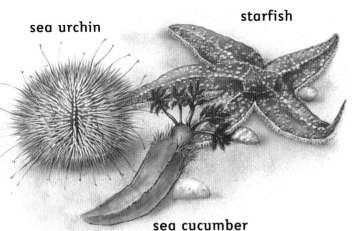

sea urchin

starfish

sea cucumber

▲ **Spiny skins**
Animals called echinoderms have spiny skins and no head! They include sea urchins, starfish, and sea cucumbers.

▲ **Tiny mite**
Mites live almost anywhere. They are too small to be seen easily.

understand

Pour water into a balloon. See how it holds the shape of the balloon. This is like a slug holding water within its body.

Animals with skeletons

An animal with a backbone has a skeleton in its body. There are several groups of animals with skeletons. They include fish, amphibians, reptiles, birds, and mammals.

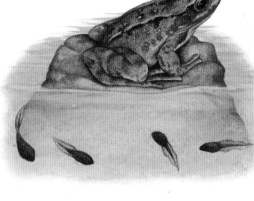

▲ Amphibians
Most amphibians spend their early life living in water and their adult life living on land.

▲ Fish
Sharks have a skeleton made of cartilage, a tough, rubbery substance. Fish called rays and chimaeras also have skeletons made of cartilage.

◄ Reptiles
Reptiles have dry, scaly skin. Like fish and amphibians, reptiles are cold-blooded.

◄ Birds
Most of a bird's body is covered in feathers. Birds are the only living animals with feathers.

word search

cartilage a tough, rubbery substance from which your ears and the end of your nose are made.
cold-blooded having a body temperature that matches the temperature of one's surroundings.

▲ Mammals
Most mammals have hairy or furry skin and feed their young on milk.

A BIBLE STORY

Noah's Ark

When God first made the world, it was very beautiful. But wicked people began to spoil it. God watched and was very sad. In all the world, there was one good man left, an old man named Noah. He lived with his wife and three sons.

1. God said to Noah, "A great flood will cover the earth. Build an ark. Gather every kind of animal and take them into the ark with your family."

2. Noah called crocodiles and lions, dogs and cats, slithery snakes and slimy snails, tawny owls and tiny wrens. All went into the ark.

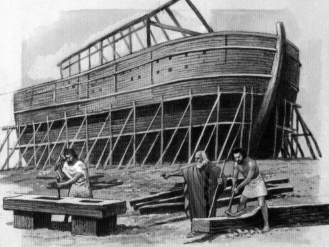

3. When the animals were safe inside, it began to rain. It rained and rained until the land was covered. The ark floated on a huge, stormy sea.

4. At last the rains stopped. Noah decided to send out a dove to look for signs of dry land.

5. When the dove flew back with an olive leaf, Noah knew it was safe to open the door of the ark. God spread a wonderful rainbow across the sky and promised he would never again send such a flood.

Why did God flood the earth?   How many sons did Noah have?

animals

What is an insect?

Would you like to wear a suit of armor all your life? If you were an insect, you would have to. The armor would hold your body together. Instead of breathing through your nose, you would take in air through holes along the sides of your body. Scientists think there are millions of different kinds of insects in the world. The smallest insects can crawl through the eye of the smallest needle. They include fairy flies and some beetles. The largest include some walkingsticks that are about 13 inches (33 centimeters) long.

▲ **An insect's eyes**
Most adult insects have two big compound eyes *made up of many small* lenses.

front wing

front leg

eye

rear wing

middle leg

rear leg

▲ **Antennae**
This longhorn beetle and other insects use their antennae *to feel the ground in front of them, to detect winds, and to smell the air.*

draw

Draw an imaginary insect. Make sure your insect has all the correct body parts. Label them carefully.

42

▲ Two pairs of wings

Beetles have two pairs of wings. The first pair form a hard cover over the second pair when the beetle is not flying.

word search

abdomen the third part of an insect's body, behind its head and thorax.
antennae the long feelers that stick out of an insect's head.
thorax the middle part of an insect's body, between its head and abdomen.

▲ Wood wasp
The long, sharp tail of the horntail or wood wasp is not a stinger. It is a tube for laying eggs in wood.

antennae

head

thorax

abdomen

stinger

◄ An insect's body
An insect, like this bee, has a body divided into three parts. These are the head, thorax, and abdomen. The head carries the eyes and antennae. Three pairs of legs grow out from underneath the thorax. Most insects have either one or two pairs of wings on the top of the thorax. The tip of the abdomen may have a tube for laying eggs or a stinger.

A flea the size of this letter "i" can jump higher than this page is tall.

Insect life

worker ant
larvae
pupae
eggs
queen ant

Some insects lay eggs as tiny as salt grains, and others lay eggs larger than beans! When the eggs hatch, most insects are small, wormlike creatues called *larvae*. A larva spends most of its time eating. When it is fully grown, it turns into a *pupa*. The insect is re-formed at the pupa stage. The outside of the pupa then breaks open and an adult insect comes out. A few insects come out of their eggs already looking like tiny adults. Others hatch as wingless *nymphs*, then develop wings.

▲ **Ants' nest**
The queen ant lays all her eggs in an ants' nest. When an ant egg hatches, the larva is fed by worker ants. Gradually, all the larvae change into pupae and then into adult ants.

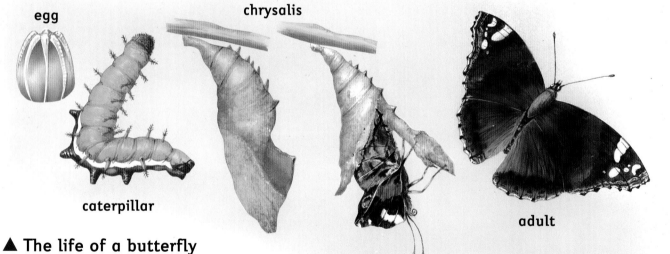

egg
chrysalis
caterpillar
adult

▲ **The life of a butterfly**
The butterfly lays an egg that hatches into a larva called a caterpillar. It then changes into a pupa called a chrysalis. *The adult butterfly breaks out of the chrysalis pumping air into its soft wings to stretch them before they harden.*

word search

larva a young insect that looks like a worm.
nymph a young insect without wings.
pupa an insect in the process of becoming an adult.

▼ Growing up

When a locust hatches from its egg, it looks like a tiny adult insect without wings. This young insect is called a nymph. It sheds its skin as it grows. After shedding its skin several times, it is fully grown.

What insect kills over one million people each year?

Mosquitoes usually live in hot, wet countries. Some female mosquitoes carry an illness called malaria. When they bite people they can give them malaria. Many bitten people die.

▶ Guarding the eggs

Most insects do not take care of their eggs. But earwigs guard their eggs until they hatch.

A CANADIAN FOLKTALE

The Fly and the Moose

In a forest was a beautiful lake. One day, a gigantic moose arrived. He waded in and began to drink and drink.

The chipmunks stopped chattering. The beavers stopped cutting logs. All the animals and fish stopped to stare. They had never seen anyone drink so much. But then they had never seen anyone as huge as this moose before. Soon there would be no water left for them. They wanted to stop the moose, but he was so big they were afraid.

"Leave it to me," buzzed a tiny fly. The others laughed.

The fly landed on the moose's nose and bit it hard. He kept on biting harder and harder. The moose bellowed and snorted. He jumped and stamped, but the fly would not give up. At last the moose charged away and never came back.

How did the fly beat the moose? Can you think of other insects that bite?

Soft, slimy animals

Have you touched a worm or a slug?

Its skin feels soft and it is covered in slime. Worms, slugs, and snails have water inside their body to hold them up. The slime helps to keep the water in. Even with their slime, worms and slugs must be careful or they can become too dry. They must stay in cool, damp places. Snails have extra help. If the weather is dry, they stay in their shells. They make a door from slime that dries and feels like paper. This protects the snail until the weather is damp again.

▶ **Earthworms**
An earthworm has a body divided into pieces called segments. *It changes the shape of its segments to move. One kind of earthworm from Australia can grow up to 13 feet (4 meters) long. That's as long as some dolphins and whales!*

▲ **Slugs**
A slug has a hole in the side of its body that it uses for breathing. Slugs and snails have eyes on the tips of the long *tentacles growing out of their heads.*

▲ **A path of slime**
Snails and slugs have a flat, muscular foot that makes slime. The muscles make the foot slide on a path of shiny slime.

▶ **Snails**
Snails may gather together when they rest during the day. At night, as the air becomes damp, they poke out of their shells and search for food.

word search

muscle part of the body that helps the body move.
tentacle long, thin part of the body, usually growing out of the head.

Wriggly wormery

Making a wormery is a wonderful way to watch how worms burrow through the soil. You can see how they slowly pull down pieces of leaves into their underground tunnels.

You will need

- large, clear, plastic jar · plastic tray
- soil from the garden · earthworms
- lettuce leaves · brown paper · plastic wrap

❶ Fill your plastic jar three-quarters full with soil from the garden.

Try covering the sides of the jar with brown paper to encourage the worms to come to the surface. Put the worms back in the soil outside after a week or two.

❷ To gather the earthworms, water a patch of grass and gently pat it with your hands for a few minutes. Worms will come to the surface. Pick them up carefully and place them on a plastic tray before transferring them to your jar.

❸ Put a few lettuce leaves on top of the soil. Cover the top of the jar with plastic wrap so the worms cannot climb out. Don't forget to make a few breathing holes in the plastic wrap! After a few days you will be able to see your worms burrowing and eating!

Eight-legged animals

The best-known eight-legged animals are spiders. Scorpions, harvestmen, and mites also have eight legs. A spider's body has two main parts. The front part has the eyes and legs. The back part makes silk to weave webs. Many spiders spin webs to catch insects flying through the air. Some spiders do not spin webs. They may wait in flowers and jump on visiting insects, or chase their prey across the ground. Scorpions live in holes during the day and come out at night to hunt for insects and spiders. Mites are tiny and live in many places, such as soil, cheese, carpets, on plants, and on the skin of other animals.

▲ **Scorpion**
A scorpion attacks its prey with a large pair of claws. It may also use the stinger on its tail.

▼ **Spiders that hide**
Crab spiders are camouflaged so that insects do not see them on flowers. When insects wander close to a crab spider, the spider attacks and eats them.

▲ **Giant spider**
The Goliath birdeater tarantula is as big as a dinner plate. It lives in South America.

▶ **Harvestmen**

The harvestman, also called a daddy longlegs, belongs to the spider family. It has a small, round body and extremely long, thin legs. It eats small insects, mites, and plants.

▲ **Spider web**

A spider hides after it has made its web. When an insect is trapped in the web, the spider comes out of hiding. It kills and eats the insect.

▲ **Wolf spider**

Wolf spiders chase and catch small animals that live on the ground.

There are more than 70,000 kinds of animals with eight legs.

Underwater animals

You may think you are a fast swimmer, but you are much slower than most fish. Fish can swim quickly because they have stream-lined shapes, bendy backbones, and bodies packed with muscles. A fish's tail fin helps the fish swim forward. Its other fins help it move in a straight line, turn left and right, and go up and down.

▲ **Swimming**
Muscles in the back of a fish pull its tail, making the tail bend to the left and right. This motion pushes the fish through water.

▲ **Seahorse**
A seahorse does not have a streamlined shape. It swims slowly.

▲ **Shark**
A shark's body is curved, which makes it streamlined and helps it swim fast. Its body is pointed in the front, wide in the middle, and narrow at the tail.

word search

coral reef a rocky place in shallow water where many sea creatures live.
streamlined having a curved, smooth shape.

How do fish breathe underwater?

A fish never has to put its head out of the water to breathe. It takes in water through its mouth and pushes the water out through slits behind its head. Inside the fish are *gills* that look like red brushes. They take in oxygen from the water so that the fish can live.

▼ **Life on a coral reef**
A coral reef is home to many different kinds of fish, such as parrotfish, angelfish, clownfish, pufferfish, and eels.

watch

Find a fish tank. Watch how the fish breathe and use their fins to swim.

Tropical water wonderland

Create an underwater wonderland full of tropical fish, seaweed, and shells. Make a boat to sail across the deep blue sea in search of buried treasure.

> ### You will need
> - large plastic jar with lid · thick paper
> - blue paint and brush · glitter
> - different colored felt-tip pens
> - lengths of colored thread · tape
> - gold paint · old junk jewelry
> - scissors · small cardboard box
> - sand and shells · green tissue paper

❷ Brush thin blue paint on the inside of the jar to look like water. Leave the jar to dry. Place sand, shells, and your starfish in the bottom of the jar.

❶ Cut out a circle of paper the same size as the jar lid. Paint both sides blue. Tape it to the top of the lid so the lid looks like water. Draw some fish on paper. Color them with felt-tip pens and cut them out. Attach long pieces of thread to the fish with a little tape. Draw, color, and cut out a starfish.

❸ Draw a boat like this one on some paper. Color both sides of the boat with felt-tip pens and cut it out.

4 Ask an adult to make a small cut in the center of the jar lid. Slide the base of your boat into the cut. Make seaweed from green tissue paper and attach it to the lid with tape. Attach the fish by taping the ends of their threads to the underside of the lid.

Why not make a treasure chest from a cardboard box to add to your jar?

5 Place the jar on a windowsill and imagine traveling in your sailboat across a tropical wonderland.

Find out more about underwater life on pages 50, 51, 66, 67, 70, 71, 72 and 73.

What is an amphibian?

Amphibians are vertebrates that usually live part of their lives in water and part on land. They do not have feathers, fur, or scales. They include frogs, toads, salamanders, and *caecilians*. Caecilians have no legs. They look like large earthworms. When an amphibian hatches from an egg, it does not look like its parents. Most young amphibians have gills and a flattened tail. They are called *larvae*. Frog and toad larvae are called *tadpoles*. Larvae grow and change to look like their parents. They eat algae and plants or tiny water animals. Adult amphibians eat insects and other small animals.

▼ **Newts**
Newts are a kind of salamander. They have flatter tails than most salamanders.

▼ **Turning into a frog**
When a frog tadpole hatches out of its egg ❶, it feeds on tiny plants. As it grows, it begins to eat small water animals and dead fish ❷. It grows back legs ❸, then front legs ❹. Its body absorbs its tail ❺.

▶ Salamanders

Salamanders keep their tails as adults. Their legs stick out from the sides of their bodies when they walk. This fire salamander has yellow and black markings to warn other animals that it has a poisonous skin.

Lie on the floor and pretend to be a salamander. Stick your arms out and do a push-up. Why do you think salamanders like to rest on the ground?

5

▼ Frogs and toads

Frogs (top) usually have moist skin and strong back legs. Toads usually have dry skin and weaker back legs.

▲ **Mudpuppies** are large salamanders that live in lakes, ponds, rivers, and streams in North America. They breathe through purplish-red gills outside their bodies. Mudpuppies can grow as long as 17 inches (43 centimeters). They are also called *water dogs.*

Many frogs can hop 20 times their body length.

What is a reptile?

If you were a reptile, what would your life be like? You would hatch from an egg with a shell as tough as leather. Your skin would be covered in scales. As you grew, you would keep losing your skin and growing a new one. In the morning, you would feel very cold and move slowly out of your hiding place. You would lie in the sunshine to warm up, then move around quickly to find food. There are thousands of kinds of reptiles. They include alligators, crocodiles, snakes, turtles, lizards, and the lizardlike *tuatara*. The tuatara is related to dinosaurs.

▲ Crocodiles and alligators
Do you know how to tell the difference between a crocodile and an alligator? When a crocodile's mouth is closed, its fourth bottom tooth sticks out.

▼ Crocodiles
A crocodile has eyes and nostrils on the top of its head. This means that it can hide underwater but still breathe air and look for prey. When animals come to the water to drink, it rushes out and catches them in its strong jaws that are full of sharp teeth.

▲ Changing color

A chameleon is a lizard that can change color to match its surroundings. This makes it difficult to find. To feed, it flicks out its long tongue very quickly to catch insects.

▼ Turtles

Turtles have a shell and a hard, sharp-edged beak to cut food. They live in many areas, including deserts, forests, grasslands, lakes, marshes, ponds, rivers, and seas. A tortoise is a kind of turtle that lives only on land. Some other kinds of turtles live mostly in water.

▲ Fangs

Some snakes, like this rattlesnake, kill their prey by using their fangs to inject poison into them.

▲ Pythons

A python kills its prey by squeezing it until it suffocates. The python then swallows the prey whole.

word search

fang a sharp tooth that may carry poison.
nostril nose hole through which air passes.

Pythons grow as long as 30 feet (9 meters), the height of a football goalpost.

Animals with feathers

If a creature has feathers, it must be a bird. A feather is made from the same material as your fingernail. There are different kinds of bird feathers. *Flight feathers* are long feathers on a bird's wings and tail. *Contour feathers* cover the rest of most birds' bodies. Some birds also have *down feathers* for warmth and *plumes* to attract mates. Birds lay eggs with hard shells and keep them in a nest. One or both parents sit on the nest to keep the eggs warm. When the chicks break out of their shells, the parents feed them until they are able to feed themselves.

▶ Flight feathers
This starling beats its wings to push itself into the air and fly forward. It can also hold out its wings to glide a long way.

▲ Eggs
The eggs of such ground-nesting birds as the dotterel have blotches to hide them from predators.

Some hummingbirds beat their wings 70 times a second.

▼ Gliding
The albatross has long, thin wings that help it glide over very long distances.

▼ Fast runner
The ostrich cannot fly, but it can run as fast as 40 miles (64 kilometers) an hour to get away from predators.

Why are hummingbirds like helicopters?

A helicopter can fly in all directions. It can fly backward, forward, sideways, up, and down. It can even hover in one place. Hummingbirds also can fly upward, downward, backward, and forward, and hover.

word search

glide move smoothly through the air without flapping the wings.
predator an animal that hunts other animals.

▲ Down feathers
The down feathers of these gull chicks help keep them warm.

Beaks and claws

A bird's beak is a big clue to what it eats. If the bird eats hard food, like seeds, it has a short, blunt beak for cracking the food open. Birds that feed on insects have pointed beaks for picking them off leaves and bark. Birds of prey, such as hawks and eagles, have hooked beaks for tearing up their food. A bird's legs and feet can also help it feed. Some birds have long legs that let them wade into deep water to fish. Some have hooked claws called *talons* that help them grip their prey.

▲ **Blunt beak**
The zebra finch has a short, blunt beak and feeds on grass seeds. It lives in Australia.

◄ **Long legs and a pointed beak**
A heron's long legs allow it to wade after fish and frogs. It has a spearlike beak that it uses to catch its prey.

▲ **Talons and a hooked beak**
The osprey has talons on its feet to help it catch fish and a hooked beak to rip the fish into small pieces to eat.

▶ **Pointed beak**
The wren uses its pointed beak to feed on caterpillars, beetles, and other insects it finds on plants or among stones on the ground.

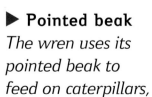

word search

talon the claw of a bird of prey.
wade to walk through water.

The tiny bee hummingbird is only about 2 inches (5 centimeters) long.

Feed the birds

Do you ever hear the birds singing in your yard? If you make this bird feeder, they will become regular visitors.

❶ After an adult has drilled the holes in the wood, paint the wood. When the paint is dry, push the ropes' ends through the holes. Make a thick knot at each of the ropes' ends. This is the base of your bird feeder. Glue the water container to the wood.

❷ Ask an adult to help you screw a cup hook to the underside of the bird table. Make a suet cake and hang it from the hook.

You will need

- piece of wood, 12 in (30 cm) square, with a hole in each corner
- two pieces of rope, 30 in (76 cm) long
- container to hold water • cup hook
- glue • paint • two paint brushes

❸ Hang your bird feeder near a window. Keep a record of your bird visitors. Make sure that the water container is full, and put out crumbs or wild birdseed for the birds each day.

Make a suet cake to help feed birds in the winter. You will need

- 8 oz (250 g) lard or fat • birdseed
- grated carrot • bread crumbs • string

Ask an adult to melt the lard or fat over low heat. Add all the ingredients (except the string). Stir well. Allow to cool. Form a ball of mixture around one end of the string. Leave it to harden.

What is a mammal?

If you look at the skin on your arm, you will see tiny hairs. All animals that are mammals have hair at some time in their life. They may have a thick fur coat, like a cat, or little hair, like an elephant or rhinoceros. Baby mammals feed on milk. They start to eat other foods as they grow. Most mammals give birth to fully developed babies. Some mammals give birth to incompletely developed babies, then raise them in a pouch for a while. These mammals are called *marsupials*. *Echidnas* (also called spiny anteaters) and platypuses are mammals that lay eggs.

Mammals for pets

rabbit

guinea pig

rat

kitten

horse

▲ **Egg-laying mammals**
The platypus is a mammal that lays eggs. The female lays one to three eggs at a time. The eggs are about ½ inch (1.3 centimeter) across and hatch in about 10 days.

◀ Caring mothers

Mammals care for their young for some time after they are born. These kittens will grow quickly on their mother's milk. They will open their eyes when they are about a week old. They will no longer need their mother's milk when they are about two months old.

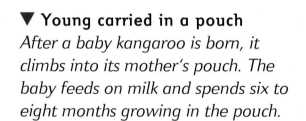

▼ Young carried in a pouch

After a baby kangaroo is born, it climbs into its mother's pouch. The baby feeds on milk and spends six to eight months growing in the pouch.

▲ Underwater mammals

A dolphin looks like a fish, but it has lungs instead of gills. It does not have scales, either.

word search

lung a part of an animal's body that lets it breathe air.
marsupial a mammal that usually develops in a pouch.

You have about 100,000 hairs on your head.

Unusual mammals

Many mammals have a furry body, four legs, and a tail. But some are different. A hippopotamus has no fur. A whale has no legs. A gorilla has no tail. Here are some more mammals that are unusual in some way.

▲ **Winged mammals**
The fruit bat has a pair of wings instead of front legs. The long bones inside the skin of the wings are like our fingers.

▲ **Armored mammal**
The armadillo has a shell made of small, bony plates fitted closely together. The shell protects the armadillo from its predators.

word search

armor protective covering.
quill a long, sharp bristles of hair.

▲ **Toothless mammal**
The anteater does not have any teeth. It uses its long tongue to lick up ants and termites.

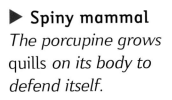

▶ **Spiny mammal**
The porcupine grows quills on its body to defend itself.

A Roman Myth

Romulus and Remus

Romulus and Remus were twin boys. After they were born, their mother, Rhea Silvia, hid in the temple of Mars. Her wicked uncle Amulius had overthrown her father and made himself king of Alba Longa. Amulius had killed Rhea Silvia's brothers, and she was afraid for her sons. When Amulius heard about the boys' birth, he sent two men to kill them. The men sneaked into the temple. They grabbed the babies in their cradle and threw them into the Tiber River.

But the cradle floated like a little boat, bobbing along on the river. Romulus and Remus slept soundly in their rocking bed. Finally, the current took the cradle to the riverbank, where it caught in the reeds. When the sun rose, the babies woke up. They were hungry and began to cry.

A mother wolf was drinking from the river that morning. She heard the strange wailing and followed the sound to the reeds. She saw the cradle and peered inside. At first, she was puzzled. She smelled the scent of man and was frightened, but the two creatures inside making so much noise were tiny. They were even smaller than her wolf cubs. Her motherly feelings made her brave. These were babies and they needed looking after. The mother wolf gently picked up the babies in her mouth and carried them one by one to her hillside lair.

Romulus and Remus were fed on wolf milk. They grew strong and were soon big enough to play with the wolf cubs. They rolled and scampered around on the hillside, watched over by the mother wolf.

Romulus and Remus were eventually discovered by a shepherd. They were reunited with their real mother and grew up to defeat wicked Amulius. To mark the spot where the wolf had found them, they founded a great city. Named Rome, after Romulus, it is one of the greatest cities in the world.

Which river did the babies float down? Which city did they establish?

In the ocean

Oceans cover nearly three-fourths of Earth. Plants live near the ocean's surface, where it is warm and light. Animals live throughout the ocean, from the surface to the greatest depths. Many sea animals have fins and flippers that help them swim. Squid and octopuses swim by pushing water through their bodies. The biggest ocean animal is the blue whale.

can you find?

turtle   shark   jellyfish   giant squid

word search

fins thin flaps on a fish's body used for swimming.

flippers broad, flat limbs that sea creatures use to help them swim.

blue whale   *ray*   *dolphin*   *octopus*   *squid*

On the seashore

The shore is where the land meets the ocean. Some shores have flat beaches with sand or stones. Others have steep, rocky cliffs. The tide comes in and goes out twice a day at the shore. It pushes and pulls the plants and animals living there. Some seaweed grows firmly on the rocks and cannot be washed away. It has flexible, leaflike *fronds* that can sway with the water and not be torn apart. Worms stay away from the waves by hiding in the sand. Other animals grip the rocks or hide in the cracks between them.

oystercatcher

▲ **Seabirds**
Seabirds feed along the shoreline on fish and crabs. The oystercatcher uses its long beak to open mussel and oyster shells and pry small animals from rocks.

Why is the ocean salty?

When rain falls on rocks, it dissolves some substances in them. One of these substances is salt. Streams and rivers carry the salt to the ocean. Over a very long time, a huge amount of salt has collected in the ocean. This is what makes the ocean salty.

▼ Shells

Sea animals called mollusks *have a soft body with no bones. Most mollusks have a hard outer shell for protection. Some mollusk shells have one part. Others have two.*

scallop shell

razor shell

conch shell

▲ Crabs

Crabs have hard cases to protect their soft bodies.

▼ Rock pools

When the tide goes out, water is left behind in rock pools. The pools are home to many different kinds of sea creatures and seaweed.

▼ Sea anemones

Sea anemones *live in rock pools and kill smaller animals with their stinging tentacles.*

word search

tentacle a long, bendy arm.
tide rise and fall of the ocean on the shore.

There are over 300,000 different kinds of plants.

In a river

You may think that nothing can live in a fast-flowing river, but you would be wrong. River moss grips stones and grows long, bendy stems that move with the water. Animals hold on to the bottoms of stones to avoid being swept away. Fish live in every part of the river. Some live in slower-moving water near the ocean. Others live in faster-flowing water in hilly areas. Mammals and birds that live in the river eat the fish.

▲ **Mayfly nymphs**
The mayfly nymph presses its flat body against a stone so that water can flow over it easily.

▼ **Leeches**
A leech uses suckers on its head and tail to hold onto rocks in a river.

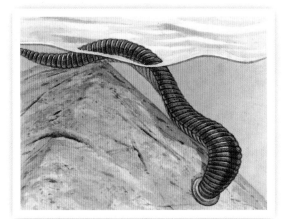

◄ **Salmon**
Salmon leave the sea and swim upriver to breed. They have to swim hard against the current. They may even have to leap up waterfalls on their journey upstream.

▼ Kingfishers

Kingfishers dive to catch fish in their bills. They also eat frogs, salamanders, and insects.

◄ Brook trout

Brook trout live in the cold, fresh water of mountain streams.

experiment

How far does water carry sand and gravel in a river? Find out by mixing some clean sand and aquarium gravel with water. Pour them down a gently sloping tray and see how the sand travels farther than the gravel. A river contains gravel near its source, where it flows quickly. It contains sand near the ocean, where it flows more slowly.

▼ Otters

Otters can swim fast enough to catch fish living in the river.

▼ Pike

Pike live in calm rivers, where they hide among plants. Then they rush out to catch other fish that pass by.

word search

breed produce young animals.
current the flow, or movement, of water.
nymph a young form of some insects.

Pond life

Ponds may look peaceful, but they are busy with life. Plants grow around ponds' edges and in mud at their bottoms. Large numbers of animals can live in a pond. They may hide among the plants or under stones, fly above the water, live on the water's surface, or burrow in the mud. Some pond animals even make their own homes out of pieces of plants or small stones.

dragonfly

backswimmer

stickleback

pond snail

dragonfly nymph

great diving beetle

word search

shallow not deep.
drought a long period of time with no rain.

▼ **Painted turtles**
The painted turtle lives in ponds in North America and feeds on insects and snails.

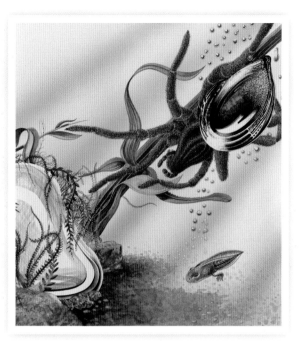

▲ **Diving-bell spiders** *trap air bubbles in hairs on their abdomen. They carry the air underwater to fill underwater webs so they can breathe.*

A CHINESE FABLE

The Frog in the Shallow Pond

Frog loved his shallow pond. Every day he looked into the water at the wriggling tadpoles, gliding fish, and slowly sliding snails. Sometimes he caught a mayfly for supper.

In his pond, he was master.

One day Frog met Turtle. He told her about his pond and how important he was. "Come and see for yourself," he said. "There's nowhere better."

So Turtle came. She wanted to swim but got stuck in the mud. She sat on the bank and told Frog about her home in the deep, wide East Sea.

"In King Tang's reign, there were many droughts, but the sea level did not fall. The greatest happiness is to live in the East Sea," said Turtle.

Frog looked at his little pond and suddenly did not feel so important.

Why did Frog suddenly feel small? What are baby frogs called?

75

Living on grass

Grass is an unusual plant. It is different from many other plants because it does not need much water to grow. In many places where it does not often rain, the ground is covered just in grass. Such places are called grasslands. Grass is unusual in other ways, too. Animals can trample it, and it does not die. When animals eat its leaves, a grass plant grows new ones. Animals eat different parts of the grass. Some eat the the tops of grass shoots. Others eat the shoots' middle sections. Still others nibble new grass shoots as they start to grow. Some animals do not eat the grass, but feed on other animals.

▲ **The steppes**
Hamsters make burrows beneath the steppes, grasslands with short grasses, hot summers, and cold winters. They have separate burrows for sleeping and storing food.

▶ **The savannah**
Grasslands called savannahs cover much of Africa. Zebras in the savannahs eat the tops of grass shoots. Wildebeests eat the middle sections of the shoots. Gazelles eat the new shoots nearest the ground.

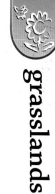

◄ Australian grasslands

The red kangaroo lives in the dry grasslands of Australia. During the heat of the day, it shelters under rocks or trees. In the cooler evenings, it feeds and drinks.

▼ The pampas

South American grasslands called pampas *are home to the burrowing owl. This owl often makes its home in burrows left behind by foxes and other mammals.*

identify

Look at tall shoots of different grasses. Find the flowers at the tops of the shoots and the leaves farther down. See if you can identify different grasses by their flowers and leaves.

word search

burrow a hole in the ground made by an animal to live in.
graze to eat grass.
trample to crush with the feet.

▲ The prairies

Bison graze on North American grasslands called prairies. They live in a family group or in small herds.

In the woods

There are many different kinds of woods.
Some have trees with broad leaves, and others
have conifers with thin leaves. In a conifer forest,
the evergreen trees grow close together and keep
out much of the light. Few plants and animals live
there. In a forest of broad-leaved trees, there is
more light because the trees grow farther apart and
lose their leaves in the autumn. More plants and
animals live in this kind of forest.

Butterflies visit
flowers for nectar.

Bats hide in holes until
it is time to fly at night.

Woodpeckers feed
on insects living in
tree trunks.

Small birds make
nests in shrubs.

▲ **Forest structure**
*Forests have five main layers of plants. From
bottom to top, they are the forest floor,
herb layer, shrub layer,* understory, *and*
canopy. *Different animals and plants live
and grow in the different layers.*

▼ Life in wooded areas

Wild boars live in wooded areas in Europe. They eat woodland plants, insects, and small animals.

◀ Nests in trees

Squirrels make nests in trees and feed on buds, berries, nuts, and even birds' eggs.

▶ Life in trees

The sugar glider is an Australian marsupial with flaps between its front and back legs. It uses the flaps as parachutes when it jumps between trees.

Wild woods

How many creatures can you spot? Cut out and paint your own owls, butterflies, and birds to live in your forest.

You will need

- cardboard box · pencil
- glue and brush · paints and paintbrush · tape
- 6 sheets of construction paper · scissors

❶ On each sheet of paper, draw trees, plants, and bushes. Paint these scenes and cut around them carefully. Glue on your animals and birds. Cut out one side of the box and a hole in the top.

❷ Using tape, attach the layers of paper inside the box, one in front of the other. Watch the light shine through the top of the box. How many of your animals can you see peering through the trees?

Find out more about forests and trees on pages 20, 21, 22, and 23.

Life in a rain forest

Rain forests grow in some of the warmest and wettest parts of Earth.
Trees grow high and spread out at the top, forming a green roof called the canopy. This makes the forest below dark and damp. The tops of the tallest trees grow above the canopy. Smaller trees grow beneath the canopy and make two levels called the *subcanopy* and the understory. Most of the living things in a rain forest live in the canopy.

can you find?

capybara   kinkajou   sloth   macaw   anaconda   giant millipede

Spider monkeys
The spider monkey lives in tropical forests in Latin America. It uses its tail to grip branches as it moves through the trees.

▲ Moths
Large moths visit flowers for a drink of nectar.

◀ Colobus monkeys
The colobus monkey leaps between trees in the African rain forest. It can grasp branches even though it has only four fingers and no thumb on its front paws.

word search

extinct no longer existing.

▲ Frogs
Many kinds of frogs, like this red-eyed tree frog, live in trees in the rain forest.

▼ Army ants
Large numbers of army ants search the forest floor for food. They eat almost any dead animal they can find.

How many animals live in a rain forest tree?

Thousands of different living things can be found in one tree. A lot of the trees in rain forests have been cut down. This means that many of the animals that live in these forests will become *extinct* because they will have nowhere to live. It is important that these forests are cared for. When trees are cut down, new trees should be planted.

Rain forest birds

More kinds of birds live in rain forests than in any other area. Rain forests in the Americas have more than 1,500 kinds of birds. Some birds help pollinate the flowers of rain forest trees. Birds of prey fly over the treetops looking for other birds, monkeys, and other animals to eat.

▲ Harpy eagles
The harpy eagle is one of the world's largest eagles. It lives in rain forests in South America. Its wingspread reaches 7 feet (2 meters), taller than most people.

imagine

What does it feel like to be a bird living in the rain forest? Shut your eyes and imagine you are flying fast above and below the trees. Write a poem or short story describing your flight.

▲ Hornbills
Hornbills live in rain forests in Africa and Asia. They have huge, often colorful bills (beaks). They eat fruit, insects, reptiles, and small mammals.

▲ Birds of paradise
The most colorful rain forest birds are male birds-of-paradise. They live in New Guinea and Australia. The male bird waves its colorful wings and tail to attract a female mate.

◄ Pittas
The pitta lives near the forest floor and feeds on insects, worms, and snails.

There are more than 40 kinds of hornbills.

A TRUE STORY

The Curious Baron von Humboldt

Baron Alexander von Humboldt was curious about everything—people, faraway places, plants, and medicine, among many other things. He was born in Berlin, Germany, in 1769. Von Humboldt was strong and adventurous. He lived in an age when huge areas of the world were still unexplored. Von Humboldt became an adventurer. In 1799, he traveled to Venezuela. For the next five years, he explored. He sailed along the Orinoco and Amazon rivers. He found the Rio Negro, a river that flowed into the Amazon, where he watched freshwater dolphins. He hiked through steamy, tropical rain forests, plagued by mosquitoes. When food ran short, he lived on wild cacao beans and river water. His canoe was swamped more than once, and he had to swim for his life in alligator-infested rivers.

Von Humboldt was often in danger. He drank curare, the poison that Amazon Indians used to make their deadly arrows. He wanted to show that the poison killed only when injected into the bloodstream. He drank juice from the cow tree, which was similar to the liquid from rubber trees. He stopped drinking the juice after one of his friends began vomiting rubber balls. Another time, he and Aimé Bonpland, a French explorer studying plants, each held one end of an electric eel to see what would happen. They felt huge electric shocks.

Von Humboldt climbed the Chimborazo volcano in Eucador. He thought it was the highest mountain in the world. He suffered terrible mountain sickness and finally stopped at a narrow track with an ice slope on one side and a steep cliff on the other. He reached 19,000 feet (5,800 meters), the highest anyone had ever climbed. Von Humboldt made two discoveries from the climb. He realized it was a lack of oxygen in the air that caused mountain sickness and that it became colder the higher he climbed.

For what purpose do you think an electric eel uses electricity?

In the mountains

As you climb a tall mountain, the weather gets colder and windier. Forests of trees may grow at the bottom of the mountain. Higher up, it is too cold and windy for trees, and only smaller plants grow. Near the mountaintop, there is little soil, although some plants do manage to grow among the rocks. At the very top, the rocks may be covered in snow. Most animals on mountains are found in the forests near the bottom. Some can live on the slopes above the forests, and a few birds can even fly over the mountaintops as they look for food in the valleys.

▲ Golden eagles
Golden eagles are found in the mountains of Asia, Europe, North America, and northern Africa. They feed on animals such as mountain rabbits and pigeons.

◀ Mountain flowers
The edelweiss is a flower that grows in the mountain regions of Europe and Asia.

word search

valley the lower land between hills or mountains.

82

▶ Thick coat of fur

The yak lives in the mountains of Tibet. It grows a thick coat of fur to keep it warm in the cold winds.

▼ Winter coat

The snowshoe hare of North America grows a white coat in winter. This makes it harder for predators to see it in the snow.

▲ Mountain goats

The ibex is a goat that lives in the mountains of Africa, Asia, Europe, and the Middle East. It has large, curved horns.

◀ Brown bears

Brown bears live in the mountains of North America, Europe, and Asia. They include the world's largest bears.

In the desert

A desert is a place that receives little rainfall. The soil is so dry that few plants can grow. Plants that do grow in the desert have different ways to survive. Some, like mesquite trees, have long roots that reach water deep underground. Others, like cactuses, can store water in their stems. Many kinds of insects, spiders, reptiles, birds, and mammals also live in the desert. Most of them stay in shady areas during the day and come out to eat at night.

▲ **Addax**
Small herds of addax move across the Sahara desert in Africa looking for plants to eat.

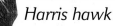 *Harris hawk*   *cactus wren* 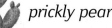 *prickly pear* 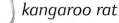 *kangaroo rat*

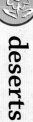

◄ Camels

Two-humped Bactrian camels live in the Gobi desert of Asia. Camels have two toes connected by a broad pad that makes it easier to walk in sand.

word search

herd a group of large animals of the same kind that eat and travel around together.

▲ Lizards

The moloch is a harmless lizard with a spiny skin to protect it from predators. It lives in the deserts of Australia.

rattlesnake   yucca   sidewinder   scorpion

Do animals live on ice?

Ice covers huge areas of the Arctic and Antarctica. The Arctic is an extremely cold region around Earth's North Pole. Antarctica is a continent that covers and surrounds the South Pole. Few plants can grow on the ice. Some animals that live in the ocean and hunt fish come out of the water and onto the ice to rest and give birth. Seals swim under the ice to find food.

▼ **Above and below the ice**
Harp seals live in the Arctic Ocean and climb out on the ice to give birth to their pups. The ringed seal mother makes a den to keep her pup safe from polar bears that hunt across the Arctic ice. Leopard seals and penguins live in the waters and on the ice of Antarctica.

experiment

Put an ice cube in a clear glass of water. See how the ice floats. Watch how most of the ice cube sits below the surface of the water. The cube is like an iceberg.

◄ **Penguins**
Some penguins live in the Antarctic region. Although they are birds, they cannot fly. Instead, they use their wings as flippers in the water.

Swirling snowstorm

This little penguin is well wrapped up against the cold. Its brightly colored hat and scarf will keep out the winter winds and freezing snow.

1 Make the body of the penguin from white clay. Attach a ball of clay for the head. Shape the wings from black clay. The beak and feet are shaped from yellow clay. Make a scarf and hat from red and blue clay.

Shake the jar and watch the snow swirling around your penguin.

2 Use putty to stick the penguin to the inside of the jar lid. Fill the jar with water, leaving space for the penguin. Ask a grown-up to wash the coconut thoroughly. Add the washed coconut to the jar. Screw on the lid and seal around the edges with putty.

You will need
- clean jar with lid
- modeling clay in black, white, yellow, red, and blue · water
- putty · 2 tablespoons of dried, shredded coconut

Why do we need wildlife parks?

Every day, some animals and plants lose their homes. This may happen when people cut down trees or take over land to grow crops. Sometimes, people hunt and kill animals for their fur, skin, or other body parts. Animals also are in danger when people take over land to build towns and cities. In many parts of the world, land has been turned into wildlife parks to protect animals and plants. Such parks protect endangered species from *extinction*. A species becomes extinct when all its members die.

▲ **Visiting a wildlife park**
Visitors to a conservation area may see animals in their natural habitat, the kind of place where they naturally live.

word search

conservation protecting plants and
animals from becoming extinct.
extinct no longer existing.
species a kind of living thing.

Animals in danger

elephant

gorilla

lion

tiger

panda

rhinoceros

design

Design and draw your own wildlife
park on a large sheet of paper. Paint
and cut out different animals. Paste
each animal on your drawing in a
place that looks like its real home.

89

Can you remember?

Now that you have finished reading about the natural world, try answering the following questions. Each picture contains a clue—the page number where you will find the answer.

▶ **1** Is this a plant? What is it called?

12

▼ **2** How can you tell the age of a tree?

20

21

▲ **3** What kind of wood is used to make model planes?

22

▲ **4** What kind of forest do these animals live in?

▶ **5** What do plants' leaves have a coat of? What does this do?

24

▶ **6** Can you name these seasonings?

27

35

▲ **7** How does a bee help plants grow?

32

◀ **8** What is this plant called? How does it get extra food?

▲ **9** What are these called and where do they grow?

▶ **10** Is a rabbit a carnivore, herbivore, or omnivore?

37

▼ **11** What are these animals called?

39

▶ **12** How many pairs of wings does a beetle have? Do you know what this beetle is called?

43

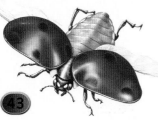

▶ **13** What insect guards its eggs?

45

▶ **14** What spider is as big as a dinner plate?

48

▼ **15** How do fish breathe underwater?

51

▶ **16** Do you know which is the frog and which is the toad?

55

▶ **17** How old are kittens before they open their eyes?

63

▼ **18** Can you name these animals that live in a pond?

72

▼ **19** What is special about this eagle?

80

▼ **20** Why does this hare grow a white coat in winter?

83

Index

This index is an alphabetical list of subjects contained within the pages of your book. Some of the subjects have another alphabetical list underneath them. These are called sub-entries, and they tell you what sort of information you can find about the main subject. The page numbers where you will find the most information are printed in **bold**.

How to use your index

subject

volume number

birds ③ **40**, **58–59**, **60–61**

Arctic terns ⑥ **39**

colors ② 43

bold numbers show where to find the most information about a subject

this sub-entry tells you what sort of information you can find about the subject

A

aboriginal people ⑥ **34**
Aconcagua mountain ⑥ **20**
actors ④ **86–87**, ⑤ 65
adults ⑤ **76–77**, 88
Africa ⑥ 11, **30–31**, **32–33**
　animals ③ 9, 74, 79, 80, ⑥ 10, 11
　crafts ④ 64
　desert people ④ **34**, **35**
　grasslands ③ 74, ④ 38
　rain forests ③ 79, 80, ④ 41
　savannahs ① 28
air ② 20, **22**
　atmosphere ① **50**
　breathing ⑤ 25
　transportation ② **70–71**, **74–75**
　weather ① 32
Alaska ④ 9, ⑥ **14**, 38
Alexandria Lighthouse ④ 14
algae ③ **12–13**
alligators ③ **56**
alphabets ④ **52–53**
Alps mountains ① 20–21, ③ 82
Amazon ① **30**, ③ 81, ⑥ **18**, 20
ammonites ① **14–15**
amphibians ③ **40**, **54–55**
Amundsen, Roald ④ **37**
ancient Egypt ① 53, ④ **14**, **15**, **16–17**, 54, ⑥ 32
　hieroglyphs ④ 52
ancient Greece ④ **14**, **15**, **18–19**
Andes mountains ⑥ 18, 19, 20, 21
Angel Falls ⑥ **21**
animals ① 9, ② 10–11, ③ 8–9, **38–39**, **78–79**
　communication ⑤ 67
　hibernation ① 34
　plant-eaters ③ **36–37**
　skeletons ③ 40

Antarctica ① 11, 26, 49, ③ 86, ⑥ 11, 18, 38, **41**
　people ④ 36
anteater ③ **64**, ⑤ 53
ants ③ **44**, 79
Arab people ④ **24–25**, **54**, ⑥ 30
Arctic Ocean ① 12, ③ 86, ⑥ 14, 22, 26, 38, **40**
Argentina ① 28, ⑥ 18–19, 20
Arizona ① 68, ⑥ 17
armadillo ③ **64**
arteries ⑤ **28–29**, 38–39
artists ④ 79, **80–81**
Asia ① 11, ⑥ 22, **26–27**, **28–29**
　animals ③ 80, 85
　early people ④ 10, 73
　grasslands ① 28–29, ④ 38
asteroids ① 54, 55, 57, **68–69**
astronauts ① **50–51**, **70–71**, ④ **31**
　on the Moon ① **74–75**, 77
Atacama desert ⑥ 18
Athens, Greece ⑥ 25
Atlantic Ocean ① 12, ⑥ 18
atoms ② **16–17**
Australia ③ 19, ④ 46, 64, ⑥ 11, **34–35**, 36
　animals ③ 75, 77, 85
autumn ① **34–35**, ③ 10–11
Aztec people ① 53

B

babies ⑤ 69, **70–71**, 88
　birth ⑤ **72–73**
　mammals ③ **62–63**
　reflexes ⑤ **46**
backbone ③ 39, ⑤ 18, 42, 43
Baffin Island ⑥ 16
balance ⑤ **51**
ballet dancing ⑤ **86**, ⑥ **25**
Bangkok, Thailand ⑥ **11**
bats ① 34, ② 39, ③ **64**

batteries ② **36–37**
Bavaria ⑥ 23
beaks ③ **60**
bears ① 34, ③ 83
Bedouin people ⑥ **28**
beetles ③ 39, **42–43**, 72
Beijing, China ④ 9
Benin ⑥ 33
Berber people ⑥ **33**
birds ③ **40**, **58–59**, **60–61**
　Arctic terns ⑥ **39**
　colors ② 43
　forest ③ 76, 80
　hornbills ③ 80
　kiwi ⑥ **35**
　nesting ③ 10, 22
　of prey ③ **60**, 80, ⑥ **19**
　puffin ⑥ 22
　seashore ③ 68
birth ⑤ **72–73**
bison ③ 75, ④ 39
blood ⑤ 27, 28–29, **30–31**, 39
blood vessels ⑤ 15, 21, **28–29**, 31
　skin ⑤ 16
boats ② **66–67**, **68–69**
Bolivia ⑥ 19, **20**
bones ⑤ 15, **18–19**, **30**
　animals ② 10, ③ 40
　ear ⑤ 50
books ④ **78–79**
Braille ⑤ **56**
brain ⑤ 15, 20, **40–41**, 44
　emotions ⑤ 61
　nerves ⑤ 42–43
　reflexes ⑤ 46
　senses ⑤ 48, 50, 52
　sleep ⑤ 68
　thinking ⑤ **58–59**
Brazil ① 30, ④ 51, **54**, ⑥ 18, 19
breathing ① 31, ⑤ **24–25**
　baby ⑤ 72
　problems ⑤ 27
　sleep ⑤ 68
　sneezes ⑤ 26
bridges ② **82–83**

broad-leaved trees ③ **20–21**, 76
Buddhists ④ 55, **69**
Buenos Aires, Argentina ⑥ **18**, **19**
buildings ② 52, **86–87**
butterflies ③ **44**, 76–77, ⑥ 37

C

cactus ① **26–27**, ③ 27, 84, ⑥ 14, 15
Caesar, Julius ④ **22**
Cairo, Egypt ⑥ **31**, 32
camels ③ 85, ④ **34–35**, ⑥ 31
Canada ④ 39, 59, ⑥ 14–15, 16–17, 38
carbon dioxide ① 19, ② 20–21
　plants ① **30–31**, ③ 24
Caribbean Islands ④ 26, 82, **87**, ⑥ 14
carnivals ④ **71**, ⑥ **19**, **22**
carnivores ③ **36–37**
cars ② **62–63**, 82–83
　engines ② 28, 59
　factories ② **84–85**, ④ **64–65**
Caspian Sea ① **22**
caterpillar ③ **44**
cats ② 39, ③ **63**, ⑤ 67
Caucasus mountains ⑥ 22
caves ① **24–25**
cells ⑤ **30–31**, 70
Central America ④ **12**, ⑥ 14, 18
Chicago, USA ② 86
Chichén Itzá, Mexico ⑥ **16**
Chile ⑥ 18
China ④ 9, ⑥ 26, 29
　empires ④ 24
　Great Wall of ⑥ **29**
　New Year ④ **70**
　people ④ 10, 45, ⑤ 10
chipmunks ① 34, ③ 22
Christ ④ **68**, 70
Christians ④ **24**, 70, 83, ⑥ **27**
Christmas ④ **68**, 69, **70–71**

circuits ② **36**
cities ④ **50–51**, ⑤ 9, ⑥ **10**, 26, 31
civilizations, early ④ **10, 16**, ⑥ 19
climate ① **32–33**, ③ 82, ⑥ **12–13**, 34
clouds ① 32–33, 40–41
  water cycle ① 13, **38–39**, ② 25
coal ① 31, **46**, ② **28–29**, 30
coast erosion ① **24**, ⑥ 34
Colorado river ① **44**, ⑥ **17**
colors ② **42–43**, ④ 80–81
Columbus, Christopher ④ **26**
comets ① 54–55, **68–69**
communication ② **76–77**, **78–79, 80–81**, ④ 53
  animals ⑤ 67
  social ⑤ **62–63**, 67
computers ② **78–79**
  designers ② 55
  future ② **88–89**
  games ④ 72
  robots ② 85
conduction ② **26**
conifer trees ① **30–31**, ③ **20–21**, 76
conservation ③ **88–89**
constellations ① **84–85**, 87
continents ① **10–11**, ⑥ **10**, 14–15, 26, 30
convection ② **26**
Copernicus ② 8, ④ **27**
coral reefs ⑥ **34–35**
core (Earth) ① **58–59**
coyote ① 26
crabs ③ **69**, ⑤ 45
cranes ② **52–53**
Crete ② **72–73**, ④ **18–19**
crocodiles ③ **56**
crust (Earth) ① **58–59**
currency ④ **56–57**
Czech Republic ⑥ 23

D

dance ⑤ **86**, ⑥ **25**, 33
da Vinci, Leonardo ④ **27**
deserts ① 10, ⑥ **13**
  Africa ⑥ **30–31**
  animals and plants ① 8, **26–27**, ③ **84–85**
  Asia ⑥ 26
  Australia ⑥ **34**
  North America ⑥ 14, 15
  people ④ **34–35**
design ② **54–55**, ④ 59, 78
digestive system ⑤ **34–35**, 68
dinosaurs ② 11
discoveries ④ **26–27**
diseases ⑤ **17**

dissolving ② **18–19**
dolphins ③ **63**, 66–67, ⑤ 63
dragonfly ③ 72
dreams ⑤ 69
duck-billed platypus ③ **62**, ⑤ 73

E

eagle ⑥ 15
ears ② **44**, ⑤ 22, **50–51**, 68
Earth ① **58–59**
  life on ① **8–9**
  magnetic ② 35
  planet ① **50–51, 54–55, 56, 62–63**
  time ④ 8, 9
earthquake ① **16–17**, ⑤ 88
Ecuador ④ 64
Egypt ⑤ 73, ⑥ 31, 32
  ancient ① 53, ④ **14–15, 16–17**, 52, 54
  gods ④ 16
Eiffel Tower ⑥ 25
electrical nerve signals ⑤ **42**
electricity ① 32, 43, ② **32, 36–37**, 39
  lightning ① 40–41
elephant ③ **36, 89**, ⑤ 32, ⑥ **32**
emotions ⑤ **60–61**
energy ① 17, ② **28–29, 30–31**, 60
  food ⑤ **36–37**
  Sun ① **32**, 52
engineers ④ **60**, 62
engines ② **58–59**, 65, 66
England ① 45, ④ 9, ⑥ 22, 24
Equator ① **34–35**, ⑥ 30
erosion ① **24–25**
Euphrates river ④ 10
Europe ① 11, 20–21, ③ 77, ⑥ 8, **22–23, 24–25**
  discoveries ④ **26–27**
  empires ④ **24–25**
  grassland people ④ 38
evergreen trees ① **30–31**, ③ **20–21**, ⑥ 14
explorers ② 66, ④ 26–27, **62**
eyes ② **40**, ③ 42–43, ⑤ 42, **48–49**, 83,

F

facial expressions ④ 53, ⑤ **64–65**
factories ② **84–85**, ④ **28–29, 64–65**
family ④ 70, ⑤ **10–11, 12–13**, 62
farmers ④ 10, **60–61**

farming ① **46**
farmland ① 28, ⑥ 22
feathers ③ **40, 58–59**
feelings ⑤ **60–61**, 62, 64, 66
ferns ③ **14–15**
festivals ④ **70–71**, ⑥ 33, **35**
Finland ④ 60, ⑥ 24
firefighters ④ **66–67**
fish ② 19, ③ **40, 50–51**, 52–53, 70–71
fishermen ④ **44**, 62–63
fishing ① 46
flags ⑥ 42–43
Fleming, Alexander ② **8**
flowers ② 43, ③ 25, **28–29**, 30, ⑥ **29**
flowering plants ③ 13, **16–17**, 82
fly ③ 45, 73
food ⑤ **84**, ⑥ **23**, 27
  energy ② **28–29**, 60, ⑤ **36–37**
  plants ③ **26–27, 36–37**
food chain ② 11, ③ 36
football ④ **74–75**, ⑥ **15**
forces ② **34, 46–47**
forests ① 8, 10, **30–31**
  Asia ⑥ 26
  North America ⑥ 14
fossils ① **14–15**
France ④ **23**, 50, ⑥ 10, 11, 25
French Revolution ④ **29**
frogs ③ 22, **54–55**, 73, 79, ④ 41
fruits ③ 26, **30–31**
fungi ③ **34–35**

G

Gagarin, Yuri ① **70–71**
galaxies ① **86–87**, 88, 89
Galileo ① 66
games ④ **72–73**
Ganges river ④ 69
gas (fuel) ① 31, **46**, ② **21, 28–29**, 30
gases ① 19, **48**, ② **20–21**
gears ② **50–51**
Germany ⑥ 23
germs ⑤ 16, 86
geysers ① **44**, ② 20
Giant's Causeway ① **45**
giraffe ⑥ **31**
glands ⑤ **16–17**
glass ① **49**, ② 12
gliders ② **74–75**
goats ③ 83, ④ 34
Gobi desert ③ 85
gods ④ **68**
Grand Canyon ① **44–45**, ⑥ **17**

grasshopper ③ 37, ⑤ 51
grasslands ① **28–29**, ③ **74–75**
  Africa ⑥ 30, 32
  Asia ⑥ 26
  Australia ⑥ 34
  North America ⑥ 14
  people ④ **38–39**
  South America ⑥ 18
gravity ② 9, 24, **46–47**, 60
Great Rift Valley ⑥ **30**
Great Wall of China ⑥ **29**
Greece ④ 33, ⑥ 25
  ancient ④ **14–15, 16–17, 76**
Greenland ⑥ 14–15, 16, 38–39
growing ⑤ **74–75, 78–79**

H

hair ③ 40, **62–63**, ⑤ **16–17**
  growing old ⑤ 80
  washing ⑤ 87
hamsters ③ 74
hands ④ 53, ⑤ **78–79**
Hawaii ① 39
hearing ② **44**, ⑤ **50–51**, 80
heart ⑤ 15, 24, **28–29**
  emotions ⑤ 61
  sleep ⑤ 68
heat ② **26–27**, 28
helicopters ② **70**, ③ 59
herbivores ③ **36–37**
Herschel, William ① **66**
hibernation ① **34**
hiccups ⑤ **26–27**, 46
Hillary, Edmund ① **21**
Himalaya mountains ④ 43, ⑥ **26**, 29
Hindus ④ **69**, 71
hobbies ④ **72–73**
holidays ④ 70
Homer ④ **19**
Hong Kong ④ 45
horses ③ **62**, ⑤ 32
horsetails ③ **15**
house plants ③ **27**
hovercraft ② 22, 68
human beings ⑤ **8–9**
hummingbirds ③ **58–59, 60**
hunter-gatherers ④ 10
hunters ⑥ 21
hurricanes ① 40, **42–43**

I

ice ① 10, 39, ② 24
  deserts ① 8, **26**, ③ **86**
  mountains ⑥ 12
  polar regions ⑥ 38–39
icebergs ① **44**, ② 24
ice hockey ⑤ **89**, ⑥ 17
igneous rocks ① **14**

immunization ⑤ 83
Inca people ⑥ **19**
India ① 45, ⑥ 26
  British rule ④ **29**
  clothes ④ **54**
  empires ④ 24
  games ④ 72
  tea picking ④ 60
Indian Ocean ① 12, ⑥ 26, 34
Indonesia ④ 26, 46, 82
industry ④ **28–29**
insect-eating plants ③ **32–33**
insects ③ 22, **42–43**, **44–45**
  and flowers ③ 16, **28–29**
internet ② **78–79**, ④ **30**, 46, ⑤ 81
Inuit people ④ **54**, ⑥ **14–15**, **39**
inventions ④ 26–27, **30–31**
invertebrate animals ② **10**, ③ **38–39**
Iraq ④ 10
islands ① **10–11**, 12, ⑥ **34–35**
Israel ⑥ 27
Italy ④ 45, ⑥ 22–23, 24

JG
Japan ① 16, ⑥ 26
  clothes ④ **54**
  empires ④ **25**
  food ④ **33**
jellyfish ③ 38, 66–67
Jerusalem, Israel ⑥ **27**
Jews ④ **68**, ⑥ **27**
joints ⑤ 22, 80
Jupiter (planet) ① **55**, **56–57**, **64–65**, 82, 83, ③ 9

K
K2 mountain ① **45**
Kalahari desert ④ **35**
kangaroo ② 47, ③ **63**, 75, ⑥ **36**
kidneys ⑤ **38–39**, 68
kingfisher ③ 71
knights ④ **24**

L
Lake Ontario ⑥ 14
lakes ① **22–23**, ④ **44**
Lake Titicaca ⑥ **20**
languages ④ **52–53**
lava ① **18–19**, ② **17**, ④ 42
leaves ③ **12–13**, **18–19**, 24
  trees ① **30–31**, ③ 20–21
leech ③ 70
lenses ② 9, 40, ⑤ 48
leopard, snow ⑥ **28**
levers ② **48–49**

lifeboat ④ **66**
light ② **38–39**, **40–41**
  colors ① 53, ② 42
  energy ② 28
  seeing ⑤ **48**
  Sun ① **52–53**
lightning ① **40–41**, ② **32–33**
lion ① **29**, ③ **37**, 89, ⑤ 33, 67, ⑥ **11**
liquids ② **18–19**
liver ⑤ 15, **35**
liverworts ③ 15
lizards ③ **56–57**, 85, ⑤ 67
llamas ⑥ **21**
locust ③ 45
London, England ④ 9, ⑥ 22
lungs ⑤ 15, **24–25**, 28–29, 38
  baby ⑤ 72
  sneezes and hiccups ⑤ 26

M
machines ② **56–57**, **86–87**
  engines ② 58
  factories ② 84, ④ **28**
  motors ② 60
  simple ② **48–49**
Machu Picchu, Peru ⑥ **19**
Madagascar ① 11
magnets ② **34–35**, 53, 61, 64
mammals ③ **40**, **62–63**, 64, ⑤ **73**
mantle (Earth) ① **58–59**
Maori people ⑥ **37**
maps ② **83**, ⑥ **8–9**, **10**
Marianas Trench ① **12**
markets ④ 56, 58
Mars ① 54–55, 56, **62–63**, 83
marsupials ③ **62–63**
Masai people ④ **38**, ⑥ **30**
materials ② **12–13**, **14**, 16–17
Mausoleum ④ **15**
Mayan people ④ **13**, ⑥ **16**
Mbuti people ④ **41**
Mecca ④ 68
medicine ② 8, ③ 35, ④ **30–31**
Mediterranean Sea ⑥ 22
memory ⑤ **58–59**
Mercury ① **55**, 56, **62–63**
  spacecraft ① 83
metamorphic rocks ① **14**
Mexico ① 53, ⑥ **14–15**, 16
  empires ④ 24
  first people ④ **12–13**
  food ④ 33
microphone ② 77
microscope ② **9**, 40–41, ③ 35, ⑤ 17

Middle Ages ④ **25**, ⑥ 24
Middle East ④ **11**, 24
minerals ③ 13, 25, 32, ⑤ 35, 36, 84
miners ④ **60–61**
mistletoe ③ **33**
mites ③ 39, **48–49**
mollusksG ③ **69**
money ④ **56–57**
Mongolian people ④ **39**
monkey ③ **79**
Mont-Saint-Michel ⑥ **11**
Moon ① **58–59**, **60–61**
  landing ① 59, **74–75**, ④ **31**, ⑤ 81
moons ① 54, 63, 67, ③ 9
Morocco ⑥ 33
Moscow, Russia ⑥ 23, 25
mosquitoes ③ **45**
mosses ③ **14–15**, 70
motors ② **60–61**, 66
Mount Everest ① **21**, ⑥ **29**
Mount Kilimanjaro ⑥ **30**, **32**
Mount Mckinley ⑥ **14**
Mount Rushmore ⑥ **16**
mountains ① 8, 10, **20–21**, ③ 82
  Africa ⑥ 30
  Asia ⑥ 26
  climate ⑥ 12
  Europe ⑥ 23
  maps ⑥ 8
  people ④ **42–43**
  rescue ④ **66–67**
  volcanoes ① 18
mouth ⑤ 24, 32, 33
  facial expressions ⑤ 65
  speaking ⑤ 67
movement ② 28, **46–47**, **60–61**, ⑤ 20
movies ④ **88**
Muhammad ④ **68**
muscles ② 46, 60, ⑤ 15, **20–21**, **22–23**, 44
  birth ⑤ 72
  facial expressions ⑤ 65
  fish ③ **50–51**
  heart ⑤ 28
  reflexes ⑤ 46
  shivering ⑤ **17**
  sleep ⑤ 68
  speaking ⑤ 66
music ④ **82–83**, 84
Muslims ④ **24**, **68**, 70, ⑥ **27**

N
nails (skin) ⑤ **17**
Namib desert ① **44**
Namibian clothes ④ **54**

Native American people ① 61, ④ **39**, ⑥ **15**
Nebuchadnezzar, King ④ **14–15**
Nefertiti, Queen ④ **17**
Nepal ⑥ 29
Neptune (planet) ① 54, 56, **66–67**, 83
nerves ⑤ 15, **40–41**, **42–43**, 44
  reflexes ⑤ **46**
  seeing ⑤ 48
Netherlands ④ 71, ⑥ 23
Newfoundland ⑥ 16
Newton, Isaac ② **9**
newts ③ **54–55**
New Year festival ④ **70**
New York City, USA ④ **51**, ⑥ 10, 16
New Zealand ④ 47, 60, ⑥ **34–35**, 37
Nigeria ① 13, ④ 56
Nile river ① **22**, ④ **16–17**, ⑥ 31
nitrogen ① **50**, ② 20
nocturnal animals ② **39**
Norgay, Tensing ① **21**
Normandy, France ⑥ 11
North America ① 11, ⑥ **14–15**, **16–17**
  empires ④ 24
  grasslands ④ 38
  people ④ **12**, ⑤ 69
  plants and animals ③ 12, 75
  prairies ① 28
Northern Ireland ① 45
northern lights ④ **36**
North Pole ② 24, 35, ⑥ **38**
  magnetism ② 35
  ozone hole ① 49
  people ④ **36–37**
Norway ⑥ 24
nose ⑤ 24, **52–53**
  sneezes ⑤ 26
nutrients ⑤ 34–35, **36**

O
Oceania ① 11, ⑥ **34–35**
oceans ① 9, **12–13**, 59, ② 24, ⑥ **10**, ③ **66–67**
octopus ③ 66–67
Odysseus ① **43**, ② **66–67**
oil (fuel) ① 31, **46**, ② **28–29**, 30, 69
  spills ① 48
Olmec people ④ **13**
Olympic Games ④ **76**
omnivores ③ **36–37**
orbits ① **56–57**, 58, 60
Orinoco river ③ 81

ostrich ③ **59**, ⑥ **31**
otter ③ 71
owl ① 26, ② 39, ③ **22–23**, 75, ⑥ **40**
oxygen ① **50**, 73, ② 20–21
  baby ⑤ 72
  breathing ⑤ 24, 29, 30
  gills ③ **50–51**
  plants ① **30–31**, ③ 24
ozone ① **49**

P

Pacific Ocean ① 12, ⑥ 18, 26, 34–35
painting ④ **80–81**
Pakistan ① 45
pampas ① **28**, ③ 75, ⑥ 18
panda ③ 89
paper-making ④ **17**
Papua New Guinea ④ 45, 53, ⑥ **34–35**, 37
Paris, France ② 13, ④ 50, ⑥ 25
parrot ⑥ 18, **20**
Parthenon temple ⑥ **25**
Patagonia ⑥ 18
penguin ① **26**, ③ **86**, ④ **36**, ⑥ **38**
Peru ④ 24, ⑥ 19, 20
pets ③ **62**
pharaohs ④ **16**, ⑤ 73
Philippines ⑥ 26
Pisa, Italy ⑥ **24**
planes ② **70–71**, **74–75**, ⑤ 81, ⑥ **41**
planets ① **54–55**, 56, 62–63, 64–65, ② 9
  Earth ① **50–51**
  spacecraft ① **76–77**
plankton ① 8, 9, ③ **8**, 38
plants ② 10–11, 20, 43, ③ 8–9, 11, **12–13**, **14–15**, **24–25**
  desert ① 26, ③ **84–85**, ⑥ **15**
  flowering ③ **16–17**
  flowerless ③ **14–15**
  food ③ **24–25**, **26–27**, **36–37**
  insect–eating ③ **32–33**
plastic ② 14, **17**
Polar regions ⑥ **13**, **38–39**
pollination ③ **28–29**
pollution ② **30**, 89
Pompeii, Italy ④ **23**
pond life ③ **72–73**
population ④ **32–33**, ⑥ 27
porcupine ③ **64**
Portugal ④ 58
pottery ④ **64–65**, ⑥ **26**
Prague, Czech Republic ⑥ **23**

prairies ① **28**, ④ **38**, ⑥ 14
pregnancy ⑤ **70–71**
puberty ⑤ **75**
publishing ④ **78–79**
pulleys ② **52**
pushing force ② **46–47**
Pyramids ④ **14–15**, **17**, ⑥ **32**

R

rabbit ① 26, ③ 37, **62–63**, 83
radiation ② **26**
radio ④ **30**
radio waves ② **76**
railroads ② **64–65**, ④ **28**, 50
rain ① 13, 32–33, **38–39**, 40–41
rainbows ① **30–31**, **39**, 53, ② **42**
rain forests ③ **19**, **22**, **78–79**, **80–81**, ④ 40-41
  Africa ⑥ 30
  Australia ⑥ 34
  birds ③ **80–81**
  people ④ **40–41**
  South America ⑥ 10, 20
Ramadam ④ 70
rat ① 26, ③ **62–63**
rattail fish ③ 8
reading ④ **78–79**
recycling ① **48–49**
reflections ② **40–41**
reflexes ⑤ **46**
reindeer ⑥ 24, 39, **40**
religion ④ **68–69**, ⑥ 26
  art ④ 80
  festivals ④ **70–71**
  music ④ 83
reptiles ③ **56–57**
Rio de Janeiro, Brazil ④ 71, ⑥ **18–19**
rivers ① 9, 10, 13, **22–23**, ② 18, ③ **70–71**
roads ② **62**, **82–83**
robots ② **57**, 85, ④ 64
rockets ① **72–73**, ② 58
rocks ① **14–15**, 16, 17, 18, **24–25**, ② 17, ③ 68
Rocky mountains ⑥ **14**
Roman Empire ④ **22–23**, 24
roots ③ 13, **16–17**, 24
Russia ③ 74, ④ 80, ⑥ 23, 26, 38, 40
  Europe ⑥ **22–23**, 25
  people ⑥ 39

S

Sami people ④ **37**
safety ⑤ **88–89**

Sahara desert ③ 84, ④ **34**, 54, ⑥ **30–31**
sailing ② **66**, ④ 74, ⑥ **30**
sailors ④ **62**
St. Nicholas ④ **71**
St. Petersburg ⑥ **25**
salamanders ③ **54–55**
salmon ③ 70
Samoa ⑥ **34**, 37
sand ① **26–27**, ③ 68
San Francisco, USA ① 17
São Paulo, Brazil ⑥ 18
satellites ① 32, 72, **76–77**, ② 76–77, 78, 79
Saturn ① 54, 56, **64–65**, 66, 82
Saudi Arabia ④ **35**
savannah ① **28**, ③ 74
Scandinavia ⑥ 38
science ② **8**
scorpions ① 26, **48–49**, 85
sea anemones ③ **69**
seals ③ **86**, ④ 36, ⑥ **16**
seas ① **12–13**
seashore life ③ **68–69**
seasons ① **34–35**, **36–37**, ③ **10–11**, ⑥ 12
sea transportation ② **68–69**
seaweed ③ **68–69**
sedimentary rocks ① **14**
seeds ③ **16–17**, **28–29**, 30
seeing ② 40–41, ⑤ **48–49**, 80
Shakespeare, William ④ **87**, **89**
sharks ③ 40, **50–51**, 66–67, ⑤ 32
sheep ⑥ **35**
ships ② **8–69**, 82–83, ⑥ **30**
Shona people ⑥ **31**
shoot (plant) ③ 12–13, **16–17**, **18–19**
Siberian people ⑥ 39, 40
Sikh religion ④ 68
Singapore ④ 51
skeleton ③ 40, **54–55**, ⑤ **18–19**
skin ⑤ 15, **16–17**, 80, 87
skyscraper ② 52, ④ **51**
sleep ⑤ 27, **68–69**
slopes (machines) ② **48–49**
sloths ⑥ **10**
slugs ③ 39, **46**
smell ⑤ **52–53**
smile ⑤ 64
snails ③ **46**, 72
snakes ① 25, 26, ③ 22, **56–57**, ⑥ 18, **35**
  sense of smell ⑤ **53**
  teeth ⑤ 32
sneezing ⑤ **26–27**, 46
snoring ⑤ 27

snow ① 13, 32–33, **38–39**, ② 25, ③ 82, ⑥ 12–13
snow leopard ⑥ **28**
soccer ⑥ **18**
Solar System ① **54–55**, **56–57**, 64–65
soldiers ⑥ **22**
solids ② **16–17**
Sonoran desert ① 26, ⑥ **15**
sounds ② 28, **44–45**, ④ **82**, **84**, ⑤ 50, 66–67
South America ① 11, ③ 75, 79, 80, ⑥ 10, **18–19**, **20–21**
  buses ④ 47
  pampas ① 28
  people ④ **12**, 40–41, 42–43, 44
Southern Ocean ① 12
South Pacific Islands ⑥ 34–35, 36
South Pole ① 49, ② 24, 35, ④ **36–37**, ⑥ **38**, 41
space ① 50, ② 9
  shuttle ① 51, **72–73**, 77, ② 58
  station ① 70–71, **78–79**
  travel ① **74–75**
Spain ④ 24, 82
speaking ⑤ **66–67**
spiders ③ 9, **48–49**
spinal cord ⑤ **42–43**, 46
spleen ⑤ **27**
spores ③ **14–15**, 34–35
sport ④ **74–75**, 76, ⑤ 89
spring ① **34–35**, ③ 10
squid ③ **66–67**
squirrels ① 34, ③ 22, 77
stalactite ① **24–25**
stalagmite ① **24–25**
starfish ③ 39
stars ① 52–53, **84–85**, **86–87**, 89
Statue of Liberty ⑥ **10**, 16
steam engines ② 58–59, 65
steppes ① **28–29**, ③ 74, ④ **38**, ⑥ 26
stitch (pain) ⑤ **27**
stomach ⑤ 15, **35**
Stonehenge ⑥ **24**
storms ① **40–41**, **42–43**
strength ④ 74, ⑤ **22–23**
subtropical climate ⑥ **13**
Sumerians ④ **11**, 57
summer ① **34–35**, ③ 10, ⑥ 12–13
Sun ① 52–53, 54–55, **86–87**
  deserts ① **26–27**
  energy ① **32**, ② 29, **30**
  harmful rays ① 49, ⑤ **17**

Sun (continued)
  life ① 8, 9
  planets ① 50, **51**
  plants ③ **24**
  seasons ①**34–35**, ③10–11
sweat ⑤ **16**, 86–87
Sweden ⑥ **24**
Switzerland ④ **42**
Sydney, Australia ⑥ **36**
Syria ④ 10

T

tadpoles ③ **54–55**
Taj Mahal ⑥ **28**
taste ⑤ **54–55**
teachers ④ **66–67**
technology ② **8**
teenagers ⑤ **76**
teeth ⑤ **32–33**, 34, 67
  care ⑤ 83, 87
telephone ② **78–79**
telescope ① 66, **82–83**,
  84–85, 89, ② 8
television ② **76**, ④ **30**, 88,
  ⑤ 81
temperate climate ⑥ **12–13**
temperature ① 33, ② **26–27**
  body ⑤ 82
Thailand ⑥ 11
  people ⑥ 27
theater ④ **86–87**, 89
thinking ⑤ 66
Thor ① **40**, ② **33**, ⑤ **85**
throat ⑤ 26, 66
thunder ① **40–41**
Tibet ③ 83
tides ① **59**, ③ 68
tiger ⑥ **26**
Tigris river ④ 10

time ④ **8–9**
toads ③ **54–55**
Tokyo, Japan ⑥ 26
Toltec people ⑥ **16**
tongue ⑤ 34, **54–55**, 67
tools ② **48–49**
Torah ④ **68**
Toronto, Canada ⑥ **14**
tortoises ③ **56–57**
touch ⑤ **16**, **56–57**
trade ④ **56–57**, ⑥ 27, 30,
  31
trains ② 59, **64–65**, 82–83,
  ④ 28
transportation ② **62**
  air ② **70–71**, **74–75**
  sea ② **68–69**
  travel ④ **30**
trees ① 30, 35, **46–47**,
  ③ 10, **20–21**, 76
  forests ③ 78
  life in ③ **22**
  loss of ① 48
tropical climate ⑥ **12**, 14
tropical rain forests ① **30–31**,
  ⑥ 18
tunnels ② **82**
Turkey ① 45, ④ 10, **15**
Turkmenistan ④ 64
turtles ③ **56–57**, 66–67, 73
twins ⑤ **13**

U

Uluru (Ayers Rock) ① **44**,
  ⑥ **35**
United States of America
  (USA) ① 17, 26, 44,
  ② 86, ⑥ 10, 14, 15,
  16, 17

USA (continued)
  cities ④ 51
  prairies ④ 39
Universe ① **88–89**, ② 9
Ural mountains ⑥ 22
Uranus ① **54**, **56**, **66–67**
Utah ① 45

V

Varanasi, India ④ 69
veins ⑤ **28–29**, 38–39
Venezuela ③ 81
Venice, Italy ④ 45, ⑥ 22
Venus (planet) ① **55**, **56–57**,
  62–63, 83
vertebrate animals ② **10**,
  ③ **38–39**
Victoria Falls ① **45**, ⑥ **33**
Victoria, Australia ⑥ 34
video ④ **88**
Vikings ④ **24**
villages ④ **20–21**, ⑤ 9
virtual reality ② **88**
vitamins ⑤ 84
Vltava river ⑥ 23
volcanoes ① 14, **18–19**, 22,
  ② 17, ④ 43

W

Washington, DC, USA ④ 9
wastes ⑤ 35, **38–39**
water ① **13**, 38, ② **24–25**
  body ⑤ 38
  energy ② **30**, 58
  erosion ① **24**
  oxygen ③ **50–51**
  rivers ① 22
  vapor ① 13, ②**20**, **24–25**
waterfalls ⑥ 21, 33

waves ① 16, 24, ③ 68
weather ① **32–33**, 34,
  ③ 10, ⑥ 12
whales ① **9**, ② 44, ③ **38**,
  66–67, ⑤ 41, ⑥ **11**, 41
wheels ② 48, **50–51**, ④ 11
wildlife parks ③ **88–89**
wind ① **32–33**, 40, ② 22
  energy ② **30**
  erosion ① **24**
  pollination ③ **28–29**
  sails ② **66**
windmills ① **43**, ② 58
wings ③ **58–59**
winter ① **34–35**, ③ 10,
  ⑥ 12–13
wolf ③ 65
woodlands ③ **76–77**
world map ⑥ 8, **10–11**
World Wars ④ **30–31**
worms ③ **46–47**, 68
writing ④ **11**, **17**, **52–53**

XY

X–ray pictures ⑤ 19, 35
Yakut people ⑥ 39
Yanomami people ④ **40**,
  ⑥ **21**
yawning ⑤ 26, 68

Z

Zambezi river ① 45, ⑥ **33**
Zambia ⑥ 33
Zanzibar ⑥ 30
zebras ① 29, ③ 37, 74
Zeus ① **37**, **43**, ④ **15**, **55**
Zimbabwe ⑥ **31**, **33**

The publishers would like to thank the following artists whose work appears in this book: Kuo Kang Chen, Mike Foster/Maltings Partnership, Roger Goode/Beehive Illustration, Jeremy Gower, Peter Gregory, Ron Hayward, Rob Holder/Beehive Illustration, Rob Jakeway, Sue King/SGA, Janos Marffy, Tracey Morgan/BL Kearley Ltd, Jenny Press/SGA, GardnerQuainton, Terry Riley, Martin Sanders, Peter Sarson, Mike Saunders, Guy Smith/Mainline Design, Nick Spender/Advocate Ltd, Roger Stewart, Gwen Tourret/BL Kearley Ltd, Mike White/Temple Rogers.

The publishers would like to thank the following sources for the use of their photographs in this book: Robert Bosch Ltd: 61 (t/r). Corbis: 8 (b/c) Bettmann; 79 (c/r) Richard T. Nowitz; 8 (c/r) Galen Rowell; 12 (c/l) Gregor Schmid; 30 (c/l) John Wilkinson; 64 (t/r) Michael S. Yamashita. Early Learning Centre: 16 (b/r). Eurotunnel: 82 (b/r) QA Photos Ltd. Frank Lane Picture Agency: 39 (b/l) F. Polking. The Hutchison Library: 69 (c/r). Kenwood Ltd: 57 (t/l). Legoland: 17 (t/r). Skyscan: 55 (b/c) Austin J. Brown; 75 (b/l) GR Photography; 75 (b/r) Gavin Skipp. The Stock Market: 8 (b/r), 35 (b/l), 55 (b/r), 61 (b/l), 82 (c/l). All other photographs from Miles Kelly archives.
Abbreviations: t=top, b=bottom, c=centre, l=left, r=right